# THE FAITH OF MAIMONIDES

# THE FAITH
# OF
# MAIMONIDES

*by*

*Yeshayahu Leibowitz*

ADAMA BOOKS          NEW YORK

English translation by John Glucker

**Library of Congress Cataloging-in-Publication Data**

Leibowitz, Yeshayahu, 1903-
The faith of Mainonides.
1. Maimonides, Moses, 1135-1204. I. Titles.
B759.M34L35    1987    296.1'72    87-18701
ISBN 0-915361-93-0 (PBK.)
ISBN 1-55774-008-9

English Series Editor: Shmuel Himelstein
Production: Ruth Eilat
Computerized phototypesetting: M. Rachlin Ltd.
Printed in Israel

Adama Books, 306 West 38 Street, New York, New York 10018

# Contents

# Translator's Note

For quotations from Maimonides' Arabic works, in most cases I have used two standard translations, except where these were inappropriate: *The Guide for the Perplexed* by Moses Maimonides, translated from the original Arabic text by M. Friedlander, Ph.D., Second Edition, London 1904, and many reprints, with certain corrections based on the modern translation by Prof. Shlomo Pines, *The Guide of the Perplexed*, University of Chicago Press, 1963; and *The Eight Chapters of Maimonides on Ethics*, edited, annotated and translated with an introduction by Joseph I. Gorfinkle, New York 1912, and reprints.

Other quotations from Maimonides – almost always from works written in Hebrew or currently available primarily in Hebrew – were translated by myself.

John Glucker

# Introductory Note

When the management of the Broadcast University and I decided that I should broadcast a series of lectures on the very wide subject of Maimonides, we deliberated as to the title to be given this series. The first suggestion was to name the course *The Philosophy of Maimonides*. At the end, we decided to name it *The Faith of Maimonides*. These deliberations, and the conclusion we reached, should serve as a token of the proper significance of the subjects of the following text.

For the truth is that, with Maimonides, one cannot separate the philosophy from the faith, or either of them from the life of divine worship according to Torah and *mitzvot* (the Law and the Commandments) – that is, of the *halachah* (Jewish Law). The very fact of the interrelation of these three constituents is what determines, for Maimonides, the essence of faith. Despite this, I have made an attempt here to distill from this unified whole elements of religious thought which may be presented even before an audience which is not wholly at home in philosophical thinking. Such a selective discussion and presentation involved us in a rather dangerous simplification: every attempt to popularize falls short of its aim. I have, however, attempted not to expand and enlarge, so as not to turn simplification into distortion and to ascribe to Maimonides things which are not his.

Yeshayahu Leibowitz
Jerusalem, 1987

# I.

## *Maimonides – Philosopher, Halachic Authority, Man of Faith*

The image of Maimonides current in the non-Jewish world, and nowadays also among a major part of the Jewish world, is that of a thinker who is taken to be the greatest philosophical thinker in the world of traditional Judaism. Such a view of Maimonides, however, does no justice at all to his true place in the history of the Jewish people and of Judaism. Maimonides has been a central figure in the world of religious Jewry for the last eight hundred years because he is the greatest authority in the field of Jewish Law, the *halachah*. The very fact that the greatest philosopher of Judaism is the man who was its greatest *halachic* authority is of an extremely profound significance.

There is an immense difference between the image of Maimonides as it is conceived in the immediate historical consciousness of that community which has been, and still is in all the depths of its being, steeped in that Judaism which finds its expression in the religion of Israel, and the other image of Maimonides which is usually the one to emerge as the object of modern research, both among Jewish and non-Jewish scholars.

Maimonides of the living historical reality of Judaism has attained a status which few before or after him have attained. He has almost ceased to be the concrete image of a historical personality and has become an institution, a stratum of the Torah in its quintessential sense – that is, of the reality of the *halachah* in the history of Israel, the basis of the whole life of the people who live by the Torah. Maimonides the man of the *halachah* has been, for eight hundred years, an immediate fact in Jewish religious exist-ence, and without him, this existence would be altogether incon-ceivable. For the Jew living in the world of historical Judaism – and this includes the Jew who lives today in the world of Judaism as embodied in Torah, *mitzvot* and the study of the Torah – Maimo-nides the man of the *halachah* is an immediate experience, part and parcel of his personal existence. The major part of the life of Torah for the last eight hundred years has been the study and discussion of Maimonides, the interpretation of his *halachic* rulings, the investigation of the sources of his rulings and the comparison of his rulings with these sources. Maimonides the man of contemplation – in the philosophical, theological and scientific sense of this term – has also been familiar to the large majority of the Torah-observing Jewish people. It was perfectly well known to each and every Jew that Maimonides was a great philosopher. But there is a most profound difference between knowledge by direct experience and knowledge by mere cognizance.

The opposite of all this emerges when we turn to most of the images of Maimonides conjured up and presented before the reader and the student by modern Jewish historical, philological and philosophical scholarship. This scholarship, in the form current nowadays, takes as its primary fact and central object Maimonides the thinker, the philosopher of Judaism or the philosopher *par excellence*, one of the major figures in the history of philosophy. This kind of scholarship is *aware* of Maimonides the man of the *halachah*, but this awareness is never turned into an object of its investigation. It sometimes includes it in the image it has created of Maimonides the Philosopher, and sometimes it ignores it altogether. The knowledge of Maimonides as the greatest *halachic* authority in the history of the Torah of Israel is never properly absorbed into the consciousness of this modern scholarship, a scholarship which is not steeped and involved in Judaism itself, but rather treats it as an object of research. Sometimes this scholarship ignores this side of Maimonides completely; sometimes it feels that it ought to find some pretext or apology for the fact that preoccupation with the *halachah* was, as a matter of fact, the main context of the life of Maimonides the thinker and the philosopher. We are familiar with the image of Maimonides the rationalist philosopher portrayed by Ahad Ha'am, who could find no better explanation for Maimonides' life-work than his sentimental attachment to the traditions of his family and his love for the customs and the cultural heritage of his people.

Such an approach would be akin to the work of a historian dealing with Napoleon, who makes a supreme effort to explain, with considerable difficulty, the importance and preoccupation with wars and armies in the personality and life of Napoleon, whom the historian conceives to be first and foremost a statesman and a legislator.

Another view which has been developed in scholarship on Maimonides – and it is represented by a number of scholars of the first rank – admits that the various manifestations of Maimonides' life and teachings do not add up easily to the popular and accepted image of Maimonides the philosopher. Some of these scholars have attempted to explain Maimonides' life-work by taking it out of the context of the problems of religious faith and reducing it to a function of political leadership and legislation for human society, something like the function allotted by Plato to his ideal philosopher.

But the interpretation of Maimonides' spiritual world as shaped by a certain conception of leadership and legislation for human society in general, or for Jewish society in particular, is vitiated by the whole atmosphere which pervades Maimonides' life-work: by the mood extending throughout that vast *halachic* material codified by Maimonides, which is usually either totally unknown to these modern philosophers or ignored by them, consciously or unconsciously; by the manner and fashion in which Maimonides deals in his responsa with problems of what is permitted and what is forbidden; with the laws of the Sabbath; of prayers, of forbidden food, of marital life; and especially his battle against transgressors against the *halachah* – one might say, his religious fanaticism in this regard. The main point which is totally ignored by this kind of

13

interpretation is the profound distinction drawn explicitly by Maimonides himself between what he calls "knowledge of the truth in its perfection" and the activities of "the leaders of states and the makers of laws."

For Maimonides, "knowledge of the truth in its perfection" is not the improvement of human society. It has a specific religious significance – one could even say it has none but a religious significance. The greatest authority of Judaism was precisely the man who was also the greatest authority in the *halachah*, preoccupying himself with commandments and restrictions which are the realization and the working out in detail of the *mitzvot*, which are the embodiment, not of philosophical speculation, but of divine worship with one's person. This fact is a testimony to the quintessence of Maimonides' philosophical thought, which is not to be found in philosophy, but in faith. Only if we realize this, can we begin to understand Maimonides.

Maimonides is the most powerful image in the history of Judaism, from the age of the Patriarchs and the Prophets to the present age, of a knowledge of God based on religion and faith. This is the secret of his greatness and his uniqueness. Looking at him from this point of view, we are led to admit that the unique place reserved for Maimonides in the history of Judaism was determined not by his being a philosopher, but as a great man of faith, whose faith found its embodiment in the worship of God.

To assert this is to deny the force of a distinction which has emerged more than once in the history of Jewish thought and which is championed even today by a number of important thinkers – the distinction between Maimonides the man of the *halachah* and Maimonides the philosopher – in other words, Maimonides the author of *Mishneh Torah* (*Yad Hazakah*) and Maimonides the author of *The Guide for the Perplexed*; a distinction which is often expressed in regarding the first (the *halachic* author of *Mishneh Torah*) as subsidiary to the second (the philosophical author of *The Guide for the Perplexed*). The most basic foundation and the pillar of all understanding of Maimonides is the synoptic view of his whole image and his whole life-work in its monumental unity and integrity – the synoptic view of *Mishneh Torah* and *The Guide to the Perplexed* as one integral whole. Without the philosophical principles which found their expression in the *Guide*, Maimonides could hardly have dedicated his life's work to the *Yad*; and without the background and world of the *Yad*, he could not have written a single chapter of the *Guide*.

This idea was expressed in the most outstanding manner by one of the greatest thinkers of Rabbinic Judaism in the last few generations, Rabbi Meir Simhah of Dvinsk – an amazing figure, combining in one person a greatness in the Torah (as part of the Lithuanian yeshivah tradition founded by the Gaon of Vilna and his disciples) and a profound understanding of the problems of humanity from the psycholgical and philosophical points of view. In *Meshech Hochmah*, his commentary on the Pentateuch, he writes: "And I have mentioned it already a few times, that the words of Our Rabbi (and for Rabbi Meir Simhah "Our Rabbi" without specification is always Maimonides) in the *Yad*, in the *Guide*, and in his Commentary on the Mishnah are written in the same spirit." This spirit is not the spirit of philosophy – it is the spirit of the *halachah*. I shall regard it as my task in these chapters to demonstrate the truth of this statement.

If I began by stating that one should not define Maimonides as a philosopher, I did not mean by this to imply that he did not preoccupy himself with philosophical thinking. It is doubtful whether we could find in the whole history of Judaism a man who thought more profound and thoroughgoing philosophical thoughts than Maimonides, and this has assured him a place of honor even in the history of general philosophy. When I say that Maimonides was not a philosopher, I refer to the significance which Maimonides himself allotted to his own philosophical thinking. To put it in a rather simplified manner, one could say that the philosopher is the man who desires knowledge. But Maimonides did not desire knowledge: he desired knowledge of God; and knowledge of God is not a part, or a detail, of general human knowledge – it is a totally different affair. There have been, in the history of human thought, men of great wisdom who have reached profound knowledge in many fields, but they had no knowledge whatsoever of God. Maimonides was not a philosopher, because the purpose of his thought was not philosophical. The difference between Maimonides and the mere philosopher is that Maimonides' aim was a knowledge of God.

It is true that some would maintain that the whole of medieval philosophy – Jewish, Chrisitian and Muslim – was no philosophy at all but theology, a thought whose whole direction was determined by the factor of faith and by the function it assumed for itself within the frame of religion. Nevertheless, this religious philosophy was real philosophy, since the majority of these philosophers admired knowledge for–its–own–sake and desired a knowledge of reality attained by man although they were convinced from the start that such knowledge is bound and destined to lead to a knowledge of God, and this faith gave the main coloring to their philosophical thinking. Maimonides' speculative starting point, as well as his whole spiritual attitude, are totally different. He does not desire knowledge in itself and has no interest in achieving it, since he attributes no value to it. It has no value for him because he finds no adequate objects for it in the reality which man discovers in his world. He finds no adequate objects for it since he sees no final and purposeful significance in the whole of the created world, corporeal as well as spiritual, including man and his material, moral and intellectual achievements. Maimonides denies significance of the whole of that reality which is the object of philosophical knowledge – and hence of philosophical knowledge itself – since he knows God to the fullest extent of the total significance of such knowledge. God is a "being" who is "true" and, when compared to "the truth of His being," what could be the value and the point of anything else which is not "true being"? (*Mishneh Torah*, *Yesodei ha-Torah*, 1:1–4) What is more: what is the reality of anything else?

More than any other personality in Judaism, Maimonides is the re-embodiment of the position of Abraham, the first Hebrew, when God tested him in asking him to sacrifice Isaac on Mount Moriah: all of man's thoughts, feelings and values become null and void in face of the fear of God and the love of God. "Fear" and "love" are the key terms in the paragraphs beginning and ending the first book of *Mishneh Torah, Sefer ha-Mada* ("The Book of Knowledge"), as well as the first and last paragraphs of the whole work. They are also the key terms in the last chapters of the *Guide*. They are the quintessence of Maimonides' philosophy, the whole of which is belief in God.

# II.

## *Knowledge of God and Worship of God*

Our aim in the first chapter was to point out a fact ignored by many people: that the main thrust of Maimonides' philosophy is to underline the total significance of religious consciousness, which leaves no room for any other values. Maimonides' thought embodies, more than that of any other Jewish thinker, the significance of the verse in Psalms 16:8, "I have set the Lord always before me," a verse which is by tradition inscribed on the cantor's lectern in the synagogue. "I have set the Lord always before me" – this expresses the consciousness and experience of a man who feels that whatever he does, whether he is – and I shall now use the words of Maimonides himself – "sitting, moving or engaged in other occupations, he is always in the presence of a great king; who, when he speaks and opens his mouth always knows that he is in the Assembly of the Great King... who is above him, and is always joined to him" (*Guide* 3:52).

We shall have to go into greater detail below as to the profound significance of the last words in this quotation. For the moment, let this formulation suffice as is. When a man feels that his entire existence is in the presence of the Great King who is over him and is always joined to him, it follows that, when faced with the greatness and sublime glory of God, all of man's values and all of his achievements are as nothing – and this includes philosophical knowledge. Here, the question might arise: Why did Maimonides devote such a large portion of his life to that very philosophical knowledge which – so it appears – is nothing more than one of the

18

attainments of man, which loses its significance in the face of the being of God?

Maimonides himself answered this question in one of his letters. A few words concerning Maimonides' letters would not be out of place before we deal with that particular one. The letters of Maimonides are different from one another not only in their content, but also – so it may seem – in the spirit reflected in them, which changes with the sort of person to whom he addresses himself. The absoluteness of Maimonides' own religious faith did not prevent him from observing the relativity of religious faith in different people, depending as it does on their intellectual ability and their psychological preparedness for religious faith. Maimonides took all this into account. When we attempt to discuss Maimonides the man and the thinker on the basis of his letters, we must always bear in mind the person to whom he addresses himself, and what he finds fit to tell the particular person, or group of persons, he is writing to. Sometimes he writes things which are not his true opinions as we know them well from his other writings. Such are some of his comments in the *Letter concerning Apostasy* addressed to the Jews of the Maghreb, or in some parts of the *Letter to the Jews of Yemen*, letters which were not written in order to deepen our understanding of the truth of religious faith, but to save a Jewish community which was on the brink of despair of its religious faith as a consequence of external and internal crises. He generally abstains, to the best of his ability, from saying something which is not, in his opinion, true – but at the same time, he does not find it fair to say the *whole* truth, if he thinks that the recipient of the letter is incapable of understanding it. But there are letters in which there is no doubt that Maimonides reveals his innermost feelings, and one of them is the well-known letter to Rabbi Jonathan ha-Kohen of Lunel, one of the rabbis of Provence who addressed to Maimonides various questions related to some of his writings. In his reply, Maimonides says, among other things: "and I, Moses, make it known to his eminence Rabbi Jonathan ha-Kohen and to all his friends the Sages who have read my writings" [and here he uses the famous expression from the dedication of

19

Jeremiah as a prophet, Jeremiah 1:5] "that 'before I was formed in the womb,' the Torah knew me, and before I came out of the womb she dedicated me to the study of the Torah and to spreading her thoughts abroad, and she is (Prov. 5:19) 'the gazelle of my love and the bethrothed of my youth,' whose love I have espoused since my youth. Nevertheless" [and here he uses the phrases concerning King Solomon, I Kings 11:1] "'many strange women have become her adversaries, women of the Moabites, Ammonites, Zidonians and Hittites.' Yet God is my witness that I have not taken them from the beginning except" [and here comes a phrase used by Samuel of a king in Israel, I Samuel 8:13] "'to be confectioners, and to be cooks, and to be bakers.' In any case, her season has been diminished [using a well-known Talmudic expression for periods of sexual intercourse] since my heart has been divided into numerous portions by all kinds of wisdom." And now, Maimonides presents these rabbis with what has been his principal life work: "And how much have I labored day and night, near to ten full years, in putting together this composition (*Mishneh Torah*), and great men the like of you would know what I have done: for I have put together things which had been scattered and strewn among the mountains and the hills, and I have called them forth one of a city and two of a family."

From the emotional tone of these words, we can see that Maimonides is speaking here from the depth of his heart. The question, therefore, is what the relationship is between the "gazelle of his love" and his "strange women." The object of his thought was the Torah, in which, and in whose commandments, he saw both the way to arrive at a knowledge of God and the actual embodiment of this knowledge – the worship of God – once man has reached perfect knowledge. But this way, the way of reason, is strewn with obstacles whose origin is in the "imaginative faculty" in man's mind, since man tends by his nature to regard what he imagines as knowledge. Thus the advancement toward the truth (and we remember that "the Lord God is truth" – Jeremiah 10:10 and *Yesodei ha-Torah* 1:4), imposes on man a critical examination of his thinking, to ensure that his advance toward God should not turn into an advance toward what merely *appears* to him to be God. "The Lord is One" – but all depends on the manner in which a man conceives of this oneness. In philosophy – especially in the philosophy he was familiar with, Aristotelian philosophy in its Neoplatonic coloring – Maimonides discovered the appropriate instrument for purifying faith of prejudices, by demonstrating that these prejudices run counter to proper faith.

We have already said that the essence of Maimonides' philosophy is belief in God. We can now be more precise and say that it is belief in God *alone* and not in anything "other than Him" – that is, in anything added to Him by the human imagination. This faith is the worship which man accords to God *alone*, and not to anything else which he raises to the rank of God. As much as thirty years before the *Guide*, in a semi-popular discussion in his preface to his commentary on *Helek*, the last chapter of the Mishnaic tractate of *Sanhedrin*, Maimonides had already emphasized how difficult it was for a man to believe in God's Godhead in itself (that is, belief for–its–own–sake), rather than to believe in Him in terms of the functional significance he attached to God, according to his own vested interest in his own position before God (that is, belief which is not–for–its–own–sake).

Maimonides' belief in the oneness of God is the fundament of Judaism: "The Lord our God, the Lord is One." But the manner in which we understand the meaning of "one" is what determines the very nature and significance of our belief. God's unity is not an arithmetical oneness, but an essential one. God is one, not because there is no second like unto him, but because there is nothing whatsoever like him: there is no thing which has any resemblance to God.

The purification of belief in God from belief in things which the believer may ascribe to God, or which may combine his belief in them with his belief in God – that is Maimonides' accomplishment in the field of religious faith. For the sake of eradicating idolatry, which could arise from a misapprehension of the true meaning of the words of the Scripture, Maimonides required the whole immense philosophical apparatus which he employed.

His words in the letter to Rabbi Jonathan of Lunel were not meant to allay the doubts of a rabbi whose environment was that of the *halachah* and the *halachah* alone; they are an expression of what Maimonides sensed and intended – that all that vast world of philosophy did not exist for him except for the purpose of understanding the Torah.

There is a brief saying of one of the Talmudic Sages which encapsules the quintessence of Maimonides' intellectual experience: "Anyone who repudiates idolatry is *called* a Jew" (Bab. *Megillah* 13a). True, this repudiation is not sufficient in itself to turn a man into a Jew – that is, into someone who has subjected himself to the Torah and *mitzvot* and has accepted them – but such a man has, at least, reached a stage in which there is a cooperation between him and the Jew, consisting of his very repudiation of idolatry. Maimonides reveals the whole profound meaning of idolatry, which consists in adoring something which is not God, raising it to the rank of a Godhead and enslaving oneself to it, whether in thought or in action. This includes any conception of the divine whose contents are human categories or values. If a man has reached the stage of repudiating idolatry, he has come to recognize that he cannot attain a knowledge of God except by an admission of his own duty to worship God; a worship in which, and in which alone, he is capable of maintaining contact with God. Maimonides conceived of this contact (*faith*) not as his view of God's relation to himself – which exceeds human understanding – but as his own relation to God: the recognition of his own duty to worship God.

This is the key to understanding the significance attached by Maimonides to the *halachah*, which is the guide to the worship of God. At first sight the *halachah*, which is an aggregate, full of details of commandments for the worship of God, may appear to be an external covering concealing the true core, which is the belief in God. In the lower strata of his interpretation of the Torah and of religious faith, Maimonides himself appears to be endorsing such a concept. But in the upper strata of his interpretation we discover that, once a man has penetrated through this external covering into the core itself and has reached that faith in God which is a total

22

repudiation of any idolatry, his eyes open, and he sees that what appeared earlier to be no more than the external garment of religion is, in fact, the true content. What we have here is a wonderful piece of dialectic, which constitutes the key to the understanding of the whole imaginary problem of the contrast between Maimonides the man of the *halachah* and Maimonides the man of philosophy.

It is true that one can find in Maimonides two aspects of faith, but these are not – as is the opinion of many people – the aspects of Maimonides the man of the *halachah* as against Maimonides the philosopher, and the contrast between them does not present us with the incursion of a philosophical, almost heretical, thought into the world of traditional faith. Both of these aspects belong inside the world of *halachic* thinking, in which *the whole* of Maimonides is to be found. It is within this world that he places his philosophy, which he never raises above the *halachah*. The distinction between these two aspects is not a distinction between the *halachah* and philosophy, but a distinction which exists in *halachic* thinking itself. These two represent the aspects within the worship of God in the study of the Torah and in the fulfillment of the Torah and *mitzvot* of which *halachic* thinking had always been fully cognizant: the worship of God (i.e. Torah) for–its–own–sake, as against the worship of God (i.e. Torah) not–for–its–own–sake. The former as well as the latter are appropriate from the point of view of religion and faith; but the value of the former is final, whereas the value of the latter is instrumental alone.

Twenty long chapters in Book Three of the *Guide* offer us a rational interpretation of the reasons for the various *mitzvot*, presented in a utilitarian spirit, as if their purpose was to educate man towards true opinions and to the repudiation of wrong opinions (the eradication of idolatry!), to the virtues, to controlling his impulses, toward an excellent organization of society and the state, and toward decent human relations – *mitzvot* designed for man and for the good of man. Suddenly, the whole spirit of the interpretation is altered, and we read:

Know that all such religious acts as reading the Law, praying, and the performance of all other precepts serve exclusively as the means of causing us to occupy and fill our mind with the precepts of God, and free it from wordly business; for we are thus, as it were, occupied with God, and not with that which is other than He.

(*Guide* 3:51; Friedlander's translation, p. 386, amended in accordance with the Pines translation)

In the beginning of this section, the *mitzvot* (precepts; commandments) are a means directed towards some "purpose"; at the end of it, they are the purpose itself. This is the dialectic in this issue: the practical precepts or commandments, the *mitzvot* which are the embodiment of Jewish religion in the *halachah*, are in the first place an instrument for educating man and bringing him to religious faith: but once he has reached faith – the "philosophical" faith of knowledge of God – he finds out that this faith has no other practical expression except the worship of God through the fulfillment of these commandments themselves. Thus:

$$\left(\begin{array}{c} \text{MITZVOT} \\ \text{(HALACHAH)} \\ \\ \text{FAITH} \\ \text{(PHILOSOPHY)} \end{array}\right)$$

To use a modern concept taken from the field of cybernetics, we can depict the relation between the practical commandments and religious faith – in other words, between *halachah* and philosophy – as a feedback mechanism. The *halachah*, which is an instrument for educating man toward faith, is then reconceived – by means of this faith – not as a means, but as the purpose itself. Maimonides' immense philosophical accomplishment has no significance other than bringing man to understand that the worship of God and the fulfillment of Torah and *mitzvot* are the very final purpose attainable by man. Let us now quote his own words in that preface to the *Helek* chapter of *Sanhedrin*, to which we have already referred:

> ...that the purpose of the study of wisdom is none other than its knowledge alone; and the purpose of truth is none other than to know that it is truth; and the Torah is truth *and the purpose of knowing it is to do it.*

These last words – "the purpose of knowing it is to do it" – are the key words. The doing of the Torah, the world of the *halachah*, is not a means: it is the end itself. This, however, can only be known to a man who has reached true knowledge; and, in order to reach true knowledge, he requires a purification of his faith in God from what is held by most people to be faith in God, and what is, in fact, faith in "something other than God."

# III.

## *Religious Faith as Torah for Its Own Sake*

There is a great and profound difference between the world-view of
Maimonides and that of his predecessors, as well as that of most of
his successors, in religious philosophy – although all of his successors learned from Maimonides and were influenced by him,
whether they were among the philosophers or what Maimonides
himself called "the ignorant multitude among people of our
Torah." For Maimonides, the world and man are not our basic
facts, which our attempts to understand and explain lead us to
derive our concept of God. Maimonides is very remote from the
kind of philosophy which aims at bringing its practitioner to a
knowledge of God in such a way. But he is also remote from what
is sometimes called simple faith. He regards this "simple faith" not
as simplicity but as cunning, since it – just like those streams in
religious philosophy – does not recognize God except as a cause for
the existence of the world and of man and as a precondition for the
understanding of the world and of man. It thus appears that both
this kind of philosophy and this "simple faith" make the world and
man, whether consciously or unconsciously, their chief purpose,
and make God subsidiary and instrumental to the world and to
man. For Maimonides, God is "true being" in and for Himself, not
because of His being the cause of the world.

This profound idea was no innovation of Maimonides himself.
He drew it from the sources of Judaism; but to many people this
side of Judaism is far from obvious. As a matter of fact, we can find
it even in our prayer book, which is apparently as remote as one

could imagine from any philosophical reflection. In the Benedictions which begin the Morning Service, we read: "You are You before the creation of the world; and You are You since its creation." God's Godhead is in no way conditioned on His being the creator of the world. Maimonides gives grounding to this pure concept of a transcendent God, the relation beween whom and the world is not that of natural causality – and we shall note in later chapters that Maimonides does not regard the concept of creation as essential for a knowledge of God. This opens before us the way to understanding a point on which Maimonides differs from every philosophy or theology current in the Middle Ages in Judaism as well as in Christianity: the eradication of the anthropocentric view; the negation of the idea of the centrality of man in the creation and the view of man as its purpose. Maimonides' thinking is theocentric; it aims at God, not at the world and man, whose God He is. The theocentricity of his thinking and of his attitude to the world cannot suffer the determination of any purpose whatsoever in the creation, since such a purpose would lead us to regard the Creator and His exploits as means toward achieving this purpose. The verse, "The Lord has made all things for Himself" (Prov. 16:4), is interpreted by Maimonides thus: "For Himself, and not for man."*

Most religious systems were unable to rid themselves of an anthropomorphic view of God through thinking of Him in categories borrowed from human consciousness and in attributes taken from the world of human values; they could not ascend to the pure cognizance of God evinced by Abraham the Patriarch on Mount Moriah, where the worship of God repudiates from itself all human values and all human conceptions concerning God, except the bare fact that He is *God* and that He is to be worshipped. This is Maimonides' cognizance of God. Any religious system which could not free itself from the anthropocentric view should have been

---

* Rabbi Jacob Moses Harlap, in his *Mei Merom*, a commentary on the *Eight Chapters* of Maimonides, notes appropriately: "Maimonides is demonstrating that there is no purpose in the world except the sole will of the Holy One, blessed be He."

dealt a fatal blow by Maimonides' position, which deprives man of his central position in the world and does not recognize in him the purpose of creation.

It is no mere accident that it was exactly on this point, the denial of man's position as the center, or as the purpose, of creation, that Maimonides has been severely attacked on two sides. In the world of Judaism itself, he has been taken to task by the adherents of the Kabbalah, for whom man was, in one way, a symbol of the divine. One of the basic concepts of the Kabbalah is *Adam Kadmon*, the Primordial Man, who is identical with the world of the divine *Sefirot*. Thus it is hardly surprising that Maimonides was severely attacked by the Kabbalists precisely for his denial of what appeared to them to be an axiom – a world created for man, the final purpose of the creation of which is the existence of man (as we find, for example, in *Avodat ha-Kodesh* by Rabbi Meir Gabbai). On the other side, Maimonides was attacked by one of the greatest thinkers of Christianity, Thomas Aquinas, who was familiar with the *Guide to the Perplexed* and made use of it for clarifying some concepts of religious thought in Christianity as well. He did, however, attack Maimonides severely for his denial of the idea of the centrality of man in creation. He saw in this denial a repudiation of the truth of Scripture – for, according to his view, the first chapters of Genesis are evidence for man being the purpose of creation. One can hardly be surprised at such a claim; for, to a Christian believer, God was incarnated in a man, and it would follow from this of necessity that man is the purpose of creation: he is, after all, the one part of creation in which God could be embodied.

It is only from the vantage point of faith in a transcendent God, who does not need the world and is not embodied in the world but in God Himself, that one can arrive at a denial of the anthropocentric view and at a proper theocentric view. Here we can say once again: Maimonides only discovered what had been embodied in Jewish faith from its very beginnings. Let us remember the very last words of the Yom Kippur service – which are, if anything, fully representative of Judaism: "The Lord is God." Nothing is said there about any functions of His.

From this theocentric view of reality, there follow some conclusions in matters of religious belief, conclusions in which Maimonides differs from other approaches current in the world of religious belief, and which created a turmoil in the world of what is called "innocent religiosity." These are things with which we shall have to deal in our following discussions, and we shall confine ourselves here to the bare mention of them. They include the denial of divine providence in the sense of a service provided for man by God, and the redefinition of providence in the sense of man's adherence to God in thought and deed. They include a view of prophecy, not as an inspiration from above, but as an attainment by man himself, the fruits of his own efforts to realize the potential for knowledge of God which is implanted in him by his very nature. When this potential is brought into actuality, a man attains the knowledge of God as a concept and as an image at one and the same time, and this is the quality of prophecy. From this theocentric conception follows also the contrast between the teachings of Maimonides and any form of "religious humanism," since any humanist moralistic view is of necessity anthropocentric – it is based on regarding man as a purpose – whereas Maimonides recognizes nothing except God as *true being*, and does not ascribe to man himself the rank of value or purpose. This is the most profound contrast between him and the great humanist Kant. For Maimonides, morality has no intrinsic and essential value; he does not regard morality as anything more than a means for liberating man from his servitude to his emotions and passions, which constitute obstacles and impediments on his way toward a knowledge of God, who is the only true being and the sole value.

If man is not the purpose, and if the aim of his position before God is not some largesse which he can look forward to receiving from God – what, then, is left to man in his world? The only answer is: in the realm of spirit – knowledge of God, to the utmost of his ability; in the realm of action – worship of God. Hence the crucial importance allotted in Maimonides' teachings to the Torah, embodied in practice of *mitzvot* and precepts, laws and commandments. Only such worship of God puts man in a connection with the true being – provided that man can understand the true purpose of such worship. This worship alone does not belong among the things called by Maimonides "the vain and deranged activities on which the great crowd of the ignorant whittle away their days and strength" – meaning by this those who struggle to satisfy their corporeal and social needs, or their imaginary spiritual and intellectual needs.

Maimonides the philosopher, the man who sought knowledge of the transcendent God, was the man of the *halachah*, whose main accomplishment was his *magnum opus* which points the way for man's religious behavior in everyday life. *Mishneh Torah* and *The Guide to the Perplexed* do not simply exist side by side, and neither of them is subsidiary to the other. They are not expressions of two different drives which dwelt together in the soul of one individual – as is believed by those who maintain that there was one Maimonides, the man of the *halachah*, and another Maimonides, the philosopher. They are one and the same thing, and they were "given from one shepherd" (Eccl. 12:11), as the supreme expression given by Maimonides to the Jewish knowledge of God, embodied in the practice of Torah and *mitzvot*.

Let us begin with what Maimonides himself begins: the four first paragraphs of *Mishneh Torah*, the composition intended by Maimonides to provide a general and overall expression of the world of Judsiam and all its aspects – as seen from the somewhat pretentious claim we meet with in his preface, that whoever has studied the written Torah and this book will need none of the books which had been written between them. The first book of *Mishneh Torah* is *Sefer ha-Mada*, the Book of Knowledge, and its first part is *Hilchot Yesodei ha-Torah*, the Laws of the Fundaments of the Torah. This title is not without its significance. In the first four *halachot* of *Yesodei ha-Torah*, which take only a few lines, Maimonides presents God, as it were, before the reader and the student. Let us read his words and analyze all that is implied by them:

*Halachah* I. The fundament of fundaments and the pillar of wisdom is to know that there is a first being and He gives being to all beings, and all beings in heaven or on earth or between them have no being except from the truth of His being.

*Halachah* 2. And if it were to be conceivable that He is not, no other thing could be.

*Halachah* 3. And if it were to be conceived that all other beings except Him were not, only He would be, and He would not cease to be with their ceasing to be. For all beings require Him, and He, blessed be He, requires neither them nor any one of them; therefore His truth is not like the truth of any of them.

*Halachah* 4. And this is what the Prophet says (Jer. 10:10): "The Lord God is truth." Only He is the truth, and no other has truth like His truth. And this is what the Scripture says: "There is none else beside Him" (Deut. 4:35) – that is, there is no true being beside Him which is like Him.

These few sentences are so full of significance and so weighty, that every single word in them is calculated and planned. The reader and the student should pay attention first to what is *not* said in these four *halachot*, which are, as it were, a definition of God. Nothing is said in them about any function ascribed to God. The reader should make no mistake in understanding the phrase "He gives being to all beings," whose significance is not necessarily that of an act. We shall return to the philosophical (Aristotelian) significance of this phrase in future chapters.

If we disregard this phrase for the moment, we shall find no clear and distinct statement as to actions of God. On the other hand, expressions like "being" and "truth" appear in these four short sentences with unusual frequency. Those who bother to count will find that expressions like "being," "gives being," "is" and the like appear ten times in these sentences, and expressions like "truth" or "the truth of," eight times. In Maimonides' presentation of God to man, everything is centered around the concepts of being and truth. This should be the starting point of any attempt at a proper understanding of the philosophy of Maimonides, which is faith in God.

# IV.

## *God as Being and as Truth*

The few words which constitute the first four *halachot* of *Mishneh Torah* are weighed and measured, and every single word in them is pregnant with significance. These four sentences speak of two things – of being and of truth. Being and truth are interdependent. *Halachah* 1 ends with the words "the truth of His being" (the being of God). *Halachah* 4 has, towards its end, the words "true being."

We shall attempt to explain these words, using philosophical terms and concepts as little as possible. *Halachah* 1 begins with the statement that God is *being*. At first sight, He is no different in this respect from other things which have being. After all, Maimonides speaks explicitly in what follows of "all beings in heaven or on earth or between them"! But Maimonides says that God is *true* being, and there is a hint here that there is being which is not true being. Maimonides also says that God is truth, and relies on the verse of Jeremiah, "The Lord God is truth." Here again, one might point out: It is also a truth to say that I am now where I am, or that the room in which I am now sitting is lit – all such statements are also truths. Maimonides, however, has said that "Only He is the truth, and no other has truth like His truth." This means that just as the being of God is not the same thing which we call "being" when it is not God, so also the truth to which we refer when we speak of God is not the truth which we know or grasp or understand when we ascribe it to any being which is not God. What is the significance of true being? In philosophical terms, it is necessary being – that is, something the being of which is derived from it being what it is, not something which only has being on account of something else. (This concept will be elaborated on below.) Similarly, the truth in reference to God is that truth which is truth just because it is what it is.

I will now try to explain these things, not in a philosophical discourse, but in a simplified manner, and will do it by using examples from concrete reality. At this moment, which is twelve noon, the statement "there is light in this room" expresses a reality and it is true. But if, in twelve hours' time, I say again "there is light in this room," it may transpire that this is no longer a truth. Thus the sentence "There is light in this room" expresses what is a reality at this hour, but what is not a reality at some other hour. Its truth is a truth for a certain time, but it is not a truth in itself. The philosopher would say: this is not a true being; it is neither truth nor being. It is a reality only on a certain condition – in our case, the condition is a certain time – and is true only under this condition.

Let us proceed and say: If we press the switch near the door, this room is lit up. Once again, we have expressed a reality, and our statement is a truth. We shall immediately perceive that the truth of this statement is greater than the truth of the former statement. Why? Because it is not conditioned by time. If I press the electric switch near the door, there is light in this room. Even here, I have not stated a truth which is expressive of being in itself, since this is still conditioned on the proper working of the electricity network. Even here, the philosopher would still maintain that this statement is a truth on a certain condition, and what is true on a certain condition is a conditional truth. It does not express a proper being, but a conditional reality, which is derived from the reality of certain preconditions.

Let us go further and say: If the electricity network is in working order, and I press this switch, the room is lit up. At first sight, it appears that this statement expresses a true reality, and that its truth is not conditioned on anything other than the things said explicitly in this statement. It is impossible that the electricity network be in working order, that I press the switch – and yet, that there be no light in this room. Yet we accept this natural reality as a given fact, without having discovered in it an inherent necessity.

The laws of nature inside our world are a given fact, but we can imagine another world in which these laws of nature would no longer be valid, and in which this electricity network would not function. The fact that within our world a press on the switch which is part of an electricity network in working order would cause light to appear in this room is accidental – in the philosophical sense of this term – and it is possible to have a world in which this would not be so. Accidental is not only a thing or an event in which one cannot discern any permanence or regularity; even a thing or an occurrence which appears to us in the world of our experience as permanent and durable can be held to be accidental, if we can conceive the possibility of its absence, or of its being other than it is.

But assume that a man were to say: In this world as it is and as we know it, in which an electricity network is constructed and is in working order, if we press this switch we shall cause light to appear in this room. Would we, in this case, have the taken the element of accident out of this statement? Here, the philosopher would ask a question which is never raised by those who are not philosophers: Perhaps the existence of the world itself is nothing but an accident, and is it possible for this world not to have existed at all? This, indeed, is a a question which philosophers do raise; and if we are incapable of explaining and demonstrating that it is impossible for this world not to exist, one can ask the question: Does the whole concept of true being have any significance? On this issue, there has been a controversy among philosophers from ancient times unto this day. The formulation of this question in proper philosophical discourse is: Is there a being, or reality, which is not contingent? Can we conceive of a being, or a reality, which is because it is its essence to be? In other words, can we conceive of such a thing whose very concept of essence cannot be detached from the concept of its existence or being?

That thing whose concept of essence cannot be separated from its concept of existence is called, in philosophical discourse, *neces-*

35

*sary being.* What Maimonides intended to state in the four *halachot* we have been discussing is that there is no necessary being except God; that in the profoundest sense of these terms, the concept of being and the concept of truth apply to God alone. Let us return to the fourth of these *halachot*, which sums it up in the following words: "And this is what the prophet says: 'The Lord God is truth.'" We should point out here that according to the plain meaning of this Biblical verse, and in the context of the preceding verses, what Jeremiah was speaking of is the nothingness of idols, who have no existence, and that he was contrasting them to the existence of God. But Maimonides discovered in these words not merely a negation of the existence of idols, but something much more profound, which he expressed in his comments on Jeremiah's words: "He himself is truth, and no other has truth like His truth." That is to say: there is no thing in all existence which is truth in the sense in which God is truth.

What we have said of the concept of truth applies also to the concept of being. Maimonides quotes the verse of Scripture, "There is none else beside Him" – the plain meaning of which is that there is no divinity except God – to mean: "There is no true being beside Him which is like Him." This is not the mere negation of any other divine being, but the negation of any true being beside God.

"Being" and "truth" are unique to God, and that is why man has nothing significant in his world beside the knowledge of God. Maimonides does not do away with the world which is not God – for, after all, man himself belongs to that reality which is not God, and from the existential point of view, man cannot opt out of this reality. For this reason, we cannot treat the world and nature with total denial, and we cannot deny man's functions or man's needs, interests, aspirations and attainments. But the man of faith who has knowledge of God is aware that all these things are forced on man by his nature, and that they have no significance of value; that they are devoid of all significance of value since they are not true being. A significance of value cannot be ascribed to anything other than knowledge of God, since God alone is true being.

As against a fashionable view current among students of Maimonides' teaching, it should be said here that the starting point of the process of knowledge of God according to Maimonides is not this philosophical analysis of the concept of the divine, the source of which is the Aristotelian doctrine of being (ontology). Maimonides' starting point is specifically that of religious belief, specifically Jewish, and it is firmly placed within a world of religious thought which conceives even of faith in categories of *mitzvot*, of religious precepts. These four *halachot* which depict the philosophical understanding of the concept of God are followed by a practical rider, in the form of the grand statement (*Halachah* 6): "And the knowledge of this is a commandment which is to be fulfilled, for it is written: 'I am the Lord your God.'" Unlike other outstanding religious thinkers, from Ibn Ezra to Abarbanel, who present belief as a condition for accepting the commandments, Maimonides includes religious belief itself among the commandments. This is the specific position of the man of the *halachah*. But, having embarked, from the starting point, on the long road leading to knowledge of God, Maimonides places the road under the strict supervision of the philosophical criticism instituted by Aristotle. He sees in this philosophical criticism the necessary means for avoiding deviations from the straight line, deviations which are likely to bring man to regard what is not God as God. Only rational philosophical criticism can prevent the man who is searching his way to the truth from falling into the trap of imaginary cognitions, cognitions which constitute the very idolatry, the struggle against which is declared by Maimonides to be the essence of Torah and of faith.*

---

* I recall a conversation I had with the late Rabbi Kook, about sixty years ago, concerning the gap between the world of faith of Maimonides and the world of faith of the Kabbalah, or between "The One God" of monotheism and of the negation of His attributes in *The Guide to the Perplexed*, and "The One God" of the Kabbalistic doctrine of *Sefirot*. Rabbi Kook, who was a man of the *halachah* and a man of mysticism at the same time, was well aware that the "True Teaching" (the term used by him for the Kabbalah) was alien to the greatest authority and teacher of Jewish law, and the little he came to know of it was regarded by him as

37

This philosophical analysis, derived from Aristotle's doctrine of being, is employed by Maimonides, not for attaining a knowledge of God, but for purifying the knowledge of God from (attaching a significance of value) to anything which is not God. This constitutes the great repudiation of idolatry.

Maimonides recognizes no significant purpose in the life of man beside the knowledge of God, since God alone is true being. The direction of man's powers, aims and ambitions toward any other purpose is nothing but toil and trouble, for no purpose. But this does not imply an intention to retire from this world, since Maimonides recognizes, in his profound realism, that man is a part of nature and that he cannot break out of nature. What is more, man is commanded not to attempt to retire and break out of nature.* But the religious philosophic consciousness directs man to negate a significance of value in natural reality – this can only be found in directing man toward the worship of God. Here, too, Maimonides reveals the depths of the religious faith original to Judaism, as it finds its expression on Yom Kippur. For, what is the summing up of those twenty-five great hours of the worship of God? Toward the end of *Ne'ilah*, the final prayer of Yom Kippur, we say: "Even the preeminence of man over the beast is nought, for all is vanity"; but also: "From the creation You distinguished man, and gave him knowledge of how to present himself before You." Man as part of natural existence, out of which he cannot break, is subservient to all the needs, to all the functions and to all the accidents which

---

absolute idolatry. Rabbi Kook recognized that the veil separating the "True Teaching" from idolatry was very thin and could collapse at any moment, and that to separate between supreme holiness and defilement was an extremely hard task which required the most wakeful attention. He therefore regarded it as an act of grace on the part of God toward the people of Israel that He gave us Maimonides, who could not be ignored by all these generations during which the Kabbalah spread among the Jews. During this period, Maimonides' doctrine of the unity of God served as a brake against the deterioration of the Kabbalah into idolatry.

* It is only in the last few chapters of *The Guide to the Perplexed* (especially 3:51) that one can detect an ascetic tone, which is alien to Maimonides' *Commentary on the Mishnah* (see the *Eight Chapters*, 4–5) and to *Mishneh Torah* (*Hilchot Deot*).

follow from this existence; but he is also to understand that although he is steeped in them, and even commanded to satisfy them, they are nought but vanity, since nothing has significance beside man's standing before God – not the existence of man in itself, but his standing before God. Here, religious value is placed against humanist and atheistic value.

# V.

## The Significance of the Belief in the Oneness of God

In the first four *halachot* of *Yesodei ha-Torah*, Maimonides endeavors to provide an exhaustive analysis of the meaning embedded in the one greatest verse of the Scriptures, the most famous one in the Jewish world, "Hear, O Israel, the Lord our God, the Lord is One." This oneness is not a numerical concept. If it were a mere numerical concept, it would not have possessed the significance which makes Judaism unique among other faiths, whether they be pagan or claim to be monotheistic.*

The significance of this "One" – and this is what lends it the whole depth of its meaning as a religious belief – is that it is qualitative and not quantitative. God is one in the sense that He is in no way similar to anything whose qualities or attributes are conceived by human consciousness. In the language of philosophy, He is the transcendent God, the God who is beyond anything which exists in human awareness, whether it be sense perception or imaginative conception.

Maimonides presents the belief in this God as the fundament of fundaments of Judaism – the belief in God inasmuch as He is God. This belief is an extremely hard task imposed on man, whose consciousness naturally tends to relate only to things which are either within his sense perception or within his imaginative concep-

---

* Maimonides acknowledges Islam, but not Christianity, as also being monotheistic.

tion, ie., to things which he can perceive with his senses or imagine to himself. If this is how a man relates to his God, it follows that he is worshipping the creature of his own senses or imagination – in other words, that he is worshipping himself. It is possible for a man to worship something other than God without being aware of this – as when he conceives of God through certain attributes which he ascribes to Him, all of which, like any attribute which a man can conceive of, derive from human experience and express a personal interest.

This great demand, to worship God and not to worship anything other than God, requires of man that he not refer to his sense perception or to his imagination, but that he *know*. The first phrase of the first *halachah* of *Yesodei ha-Torah* after the introductory words "The fundament of fundaments and the pillar of wisdom," is "to know." It is the duty of man *to know* that "there is none else beside Him." But this is not to say that Maimonides does not regard the world as real, like certain streams in mysticism which consider the whole world merely as a symbol of a true reality. For Maimonides the world is no symbol, and its existence is no illusion of human awareness; it is an objective reality, albeit no true being in the philosophical sense of this term. But if a man regards the world perceived by his senses as true being, and his own existence in the world as a true value, at the same time laying a claim to belief in God as the creator and sustainer of the world, then he is mistaken. Such a man really does not believe in God but in a world of which God is the Lord. In other words, the world, including himself, becomes for him a purpose, and God becomes for him a means for this purpose. But the God of pure monotheism is not God for the sake of the world, neither from the ontological point of view – for the sake of the existence of the world – nor from the epistemological point of view – for the sake of man's understanding of the world.

Here we have touched on the distinction between two conceptions of religious belief, and understanding this distinction is the key to understanding Maimonides' doctrine of faith. It is obvious that Maimonides distinguishes between two layers of belief; but this is not – as some of his modern commentators think – a distinction between faith as reflected in the world of *halachah* and faith as conceived by philosophy, but a distinction which is wholly within the world of the *halachah*, which draws the line between *Torah for–its–own–sake* and *Torah not–for–its–own–sake.*"

Maimonides is fully aware that even worship of God not–for–its–own–sake, but which originates in man's believing in God because he is in need of such a belief for giving ground to his existence or for understanding the world – even such religiosity is permissible. In the introduction to the *Helek* chapter of *Sanhedrin*, to which we have already referred, he maintains that the Talmudic Sages had already realized that not every man is capable of Torah for–its–own–sake, whose origin is in a knowledge of God *qua* God, rather than through functions ascribed to Him in relation to the world and the believer himself. Man was therefore *permitted* "to worship God and fulfill the commandments for the hope of reward and to abstain from prohibitions for fear of punishment." But this is not the purpose of the Torah. The true significance of faith is *to know the truth because it is truth*. Maimonides' saying in the introduction to *Helek*, "The purpose of truth is none other than to know the truth," appears at first sight as a general principle of axiology (the theory of value), with no particular religious significance. Many non-religious thinkers and moralists would agree with Maimonides that one should know the truth because it is truth – that is, not because it is useful; not because it gives us additional power and strength and potentialities, but because it is the truth. But if we put together this saying in the introduction to *Helek* with the first four *halachot* of *Mishneh Torah*, we shall understand this saying in a completely different sense. It is then turned from an axiological and moral principle to a principle of religious faith; if "the Lord God is truth," and "Only He is truth, and no other has truth like His truth," and there is no true being beside Him which is like Him" – then knowledge of truth is nothing but knowledge of God, and knowledge of truth because it is truth is nothing but the belief in God because of His divinity and not for any consequences of this belief. This belief involves the recognition of our duty to worship God: "... and the Torah is true, and the purpose of its knowledge is to do it." In this context, Maimonides presents, as an archetype of faith, the Patriarch Abraham. "Take now your son..." (Genesis 22:2 ff.) is a command which no man could possibly fulfill if he conceived of God in human categories and values (the judge of all earth, the rewarder and punisher, a God of justice, mercy, and the like). The fulfillment of this command requires a repudiation of all human values, and even of all human goals (God's covenant with Abraham, which involves Isaac) before one's duty to God. There is no reward which can be given for fulfilling such a command, unless the man who fulfills it regards it – that is, the unconditional worship of God – as the reward itself. This is the worship of God *for–its–own–sake*, which is called *love* ("And you shall love the Lord... with all your heart and with all your soul and with all your might"), and it was Abraham who had the privilege to be called "the one who loved God" (Isaiah 41:8, in the Hebrew original).

The whole extensive philosophical apparatus employed by Maimonides has only the single purpose of reducing the knowledge of God to the knowledge of his *Godness* through the removal of any corporeality or anthropomorphism from the belief in God. This is the belief in the oneness of God, from which follows the negation of attributes which are of necessity derived from man's experience and consciousness. Man may only attain this knowledge after he has succeeded in overcoming his imaginative faculty through the faculty of his intellect. For it is the imaginative faculty which nourishes the passions and drives which tie man to things "other than God." This is the kind of knowledge of God which was attained by Moses. This is the meaning of the grand things said about Moses: "And the Lord spoke unto Moses face to face, as a man speaks unto his friend" (Exodus 33:11); "With him will I speak mouth to mouth, openly, and not in riddles, and the similitude of the Lord shall he behold" (Numbers 12:8); "whom the Lord knew face to face" (Deuteronomy 34:10). All these expressions, which look like statements about God, are really only statements about Moses. Moses had removed most of the "partitions" which separate the human intellect from the knowledge of God, and "There remained between Moses and the comprehension of the true essence of God only one transparent obstruction" (*Eight Chapters* 7) – that is, his being human. Moses was the perfect man, in whom true knowledge of God, as far as it is possible for man, was embodied.

Just as the love of God embodied in Abraham was love for–its–own-sake, so is the pure intellectual knowledge of God which was embodied in Moses a love of God: "A man does not love God except in the knowledge he has of Him, and as the knowledge is, so is the love" (*Mishneh Torah, Hilchot Teshuvah*). In all his works – in his commentary on the Mishnah (*Helek*), in *Mishneh Torah* (*Yesodei ha–Torah* 7), and time and again in *The Guide to the Perplexed* – Maimonides presents Moses as the elect of the human race. Hence, some of Maimonides' commentators found support for their view that Maimonides places knowledge of God (in the sense of philosophy) above worship of God (in the sense of *mitzvot* – that is, the *halachah*). This is not so. It is true that for Maimonides knowledge of God is the supreme value as far as human perfection is concerned, but it is not, for him, man's existential purpose. Philosophical knowledge of God purifies our belief in God from the belief in "other than God"; but its concrete realization is not in itself alone, but in its leading man toward worshipping God in true worship – worship for–its–own-sake. The world of *mitzvot* and the *halachah* is not, for Maimonides, inferior to the world of philosophy, nor is it parallel to the world of philosophy: it is that thing toward which philosophical knowledge directs man.

# VI.

## Knowledge of God as a Commandment

The great religious principle embodied in the first four *halachot* of *Mishneh Torah* is presented without any attempt to verify it, to prove it, or to adduce a demonstration for it. At the same time, it is well known to anyone who has contemplated Maimonides' world, and to anyone engaged in the history of philosophical thought and familiar with Maimonides' place in the history of philosophy, that one of the chief constituents of Maimonides' thought is the preoccupation with finding "proofs" for the existence of God. This, too, is one of the things which sometimes tend to mislead those commentators on Maimonides who are not at home in the world of faith of Torah and *mitzvot*, of which Maimonides was part and parcel. They reach the mistaken conclusion that Maimonides' God is the God which philosophical thinking leads man to recognize.

In these four *halachot*, God is not in any way presented as one whose knowledge we reach by philosophical cognition; rather, the first presupposition is that He is already known, that man knows that there is God, and all that is required of him is that he should make no mistake in his interpretation of this knowledge, and that he should not turn his faith in God into a belief in idols. What, then, is the significance of the vast array of philosophical discussions in *The Guide to the Perplexed* which deal with demonstrations of the existence of God? That will be the subject of another chapter. Here, we shall concentrate on the large issue of *belief*.

Soon after the summarizing of the four philosophical *halachot*, which is the statement that there is no true being but God, we are told in *halachah* 6: "And knowledge of this is a practical commandment (*mitzvat aseh*); for it is written: I am the Lord your God." These few words open before us wide avenues of thought. There are many – and they include some of the greatest thinkers and believers in Judaism, and more so among the Gentiles, and even more so among scholars and thinkers who are not men of faith themselves, but are only preoccupied with the historical human phenomenon called religious faith – among whom the accepted view is that the whole array of the commandments, the *mitzvot* (or, to be precise, the acceptance of these *mitzvot* by man), is derived from a man's faith. A man's faith, they believe, originates in intellectual or psychological and emotional factors, and these, in turn, are derived from a man's involuntary attitude to cosmic reality, to the heavens and the earth and all their hosts, and needless to say, to other people and to himself. That is to say, a man arrives at the idea of the existence of God from the reality which he perceives or imagines and attempts to understand, and from this concept of God he is likely to arrive at the concept of a God who imposes on him *mitzvot* which are binding on him.

Maimonides, however, knows that the knowledge of the existence of God is itself a *mitzvah*, and he links it to the first words of the Ten Commandments. Here we meet with a very interesting phenomenon. What is called, in Jewish religious and literary tradition, the First Commandment, does not have the form of a commandment. The commandments actually begin with "You shall have no other gods before me"; but are preceded by "I am the Lord God, who has brought you out of the land of Egypt, out of the house of bondage." Maimonides counts this as the First Commandment; but some of the greatest religious thinkers in Judaism maintain that "You shall have no other gods before me" is the First Commandment proper, whereas "I am..." is only a declaration, which cannot be counted amongst the commandments, since it is a precondition for regarding the following statements as God's commandments.

It follows from this conception that belief in the existence of God is itself beyond religion, as far as religion is defined by the network of commandments for the worship of God. This is a supposition which Maimonides is in no way prepared to accept. For him, knowledge of God is itself one of the commandments binding on man. This means that religious belief has none but a religious basis, not a philosophical one. Man does not reach knowledge of God – and, through it, the fulfillment of His commandments – because he knows something about the heavens and the earth and all their hosts, about nature and history. If this were the case, it would follow that there is something beyond and outside the belief in God, and that this something is what brings us to belief in God.

For Maimonides, there is no truth beside God himself: "There is none else beside Him." Thus, it is impossible that there should be anything outside knowledge of God which could lead us to knowledge of God. Therefore, Maimonides asserts: "And knowledge of this is a practical commandment" – a commandment which is not prior to the acceptance of God's commandments, or a condition for their acceptance, but is itself a constituent of the religious commandments, and their chief constituent: "I am the Lord your God."

Something similar is done by that second great figure in medieval Jewish religious thought, Judah Halevi. When he makes his Scholar explain to the King of the Khazars the principles of Jewish faith, he begins with "I am the Lord your God, who has brought you out of the land of Egypt." On the face of it, this is identical to Maimonides' position. But whereas to Judah Halevi the *second* half of this verse, "who has brought you out of the land of Egypt, out of the house of bondage," is the significant part of the verse, for Maimonides, the first few words, "I am the Lord your God," are the key words, and it is quite intentionally that he does not refer in this context to the second half of the verse, "who has brought you out of the land of Egypt, out of the house of bondage." For Judah Halevi, God is conceived through history: we believe in God who has revealed Himself to us within the historical reality of our people. Maimonides, in this context, omits the second half of this verse, although there is not the slightest doubt that he was as familiar with it and cognizant of it as was Rabbi Judah Halevi: he does not regard it as the foundation of religious belief. Everything that has happened in history, including the revelation of God in historical events, is only a matter of man's destiny, of man's memories and of man's expectations of the future. Had Maimonides ever discussed the *Kuzari*, he would have said that Rabbi Judah Halevi's faith is a faith not–for–its–own–sake, a faith taken as a human value. For Halevi, this value is embodied in the destiny of the people of Israel, which is, in a certain sense, the representative of true humanity. But if God is to be conceived in terms of His relation to the people of Israel and to the history of the people of Israel, it follows that belief in this God is – for Maimonides – a belief not–for–its–own–sake. In the whole of *Hilchot Yesodei ha-Torah*, the *Halachot Concerning the Foundations of the Torah*, the historical destiny of the people of Israel is never even mentioned. Even the word "Israel" – the fundamental principle in the world of thought of Rabbi Judah Halevi – is never mentioned in the first four chapters of *Yesodei ha–Torah*, which deal with the doctrine of God, the doctrine of the cosmos and the doctrine of man. It appears suddenly in the first *halachah* of Chapter Five: "The whole of the House of Israel is commanded to sanctify the great Name of God..." Knowledge of God (like knowledge of the world and of man himself) is a task incumbent on man *qua* man: the unique religious position of *Jewish man* is *the commandments*.

One should not for a moment imagine that Maimonides was less attached to the people of Israel and to the destiny of Israel than Judah Halevi, or that the significance of the people of Israel for Maimonides was inferior to the significance of the people of Israel for Judah Halevi. But as far as Maimonides' idea of knowledge of God is concerned, even the people of Israel, its historical destiny and its mission are not fundaments of religious belief. The fundament of belief in God is God himself. The knowledge that there is a first being, that there is no truth like the truth of His being, that He is true being, and that there is none beside Him – this is a commandment of God, not something which man arrives at through a knowledge of the history and mission of the people of Israel, but through knowing God because He is God, and being aware that this knowledge is the command of God. The profound depth of Maimonides' faith is revealed by the fact that for him, cognizance of God is not a condition leading to the worship of God and the acceptance of His commandments, but that it is in itself a commandment. Why do I believe in God? Because it is a *mitzvah*, a commandment, to believe in God.

The many long chapters of *The Guide to the Perplexed* whose object is the "demonstration" of the existence of God, that is, the logical and deductive proofs of His being, should not be seen as the foundation on which one is to erect the edifice of faith, but as clarifying to man his belief in God. A man who does not believe in God is not very likely to be convinced to believe through the four considerations which constitute for Maimonides the demonstrations of the existence of God. But if a man believes in God, these demonstrations will clarify for him what can be said of the existence of God and what cannot be said about it, so as to make his faith an intellectual faith in God, not in something conceived as God in man's imaginative and emotional awareness.

On this issue, opinions have been divided among Maimonides' commentators. Some of them, both from among the believers and those who are devoid of religious belief, have seen the vast religious apparatus employed for proving the existence of God as the foundation of Maimonides' faith. According to this view, his faith is a conclusion derived from the world of his philosophical thought. This approach seems to me to be erroneous, if we consider the fact that Maimonides' discussion of these philosophical demonstrations begins with a polemic against a theological system which was popular in Maimonides' cultural milieu, the milieu of Islamic religious philosophy. I refer to the theological system of the *Kalam*, which was based on a knowledge of God derived from a certain conception of the universe. The *Kalam* attempted to prove, from an observation of the world, that the world is not eternal – that is, that it does not possess an everlasting existence involved in its very essence, but that it is created – that is, that it has a beginning in time. In other words, it was made or created, and thus it follows of necessity that someone created it – since nothing creates itself – and this creator and maker of the world is God.

Maimonides rejects the *Kalam*'s system of demonstrating the existence of God. He does it both for reasons of philosophical speculation and for reasons of religious faith. We shall not enlarge here on Maimonides' philosophical criticism of the *Kalam*, whose foundations – and therefore also conclusions – he finds to be undermined by the principles of Aristotelian metaphysics and by his criteria of philosophical thinking. In the light of these criteria, the conclusion drawn by the *Kalam* from the world as it is now to the creation of the world is logically invalid. But far greater significance, as far as understanding the essence of Maimonides' religious faith is concerned, is to be attached to his staunch opposition to the *Kalam* view which makes belief in God conditional on recognition of the creation of the universe. This is a "belief dependent upon some external cause" – which, like the "love dependent upon an external cause" (*Mishnah Avot* 5:19), "passes away with the passing away of that cause." The *Kalam* turns the belief in God into an instrument for man to help him understand the existence of the world; but a man who reaches his belief through this avenue does not believe in the divinity of God, but in His function as a creator. It follows that he makes the world a purpose and makes God a means to that purpose. This is an instrumental God, whose essence is the function He fulfills in relation to the world or in enabling man to understand the world. This is a cognizance of God which implies degradation of the true significance of the idea of God in proper religious faith. It is against this kind of approach that Maimonides directs the third of the four *halachot* which open *Mishneh Torah*: "And if it were to be conceived that all other beings except Him were not, Only He would be..." Knowledge of God is not to be conditional on His being God of the world; knowledge of God consists in recognizing Him as God.

Maimonides takes upon himself the great task of verifying the existence of God by way of deductive reasoning, by means of demonstrations, the validity of which is not conditional upon any presupposition as to the eternity or creation of the world. Even if it is impossible to demonstrate that the world is "new" – that is, that it had a beginning in time – man can, and is also bound, to believe in God on the basis of a discussion of the world as it is (that is, as it is known to us from Aristotle's physics, cosmology and ontology), and through drawing necessary conclusions (according to Aristotle's logic and epistemology) from the nature of thinking itself. This approach of Maimonides appears to be shocking to many sincere believers, whose faith in God centers on His being the creator of the universe. For Maimonides, God is God independently of the problem of the creation of the universe.

As against a current view, one should point out that this is not "philosophical religiosity" as opposed to "naive faith," but this is itself religious faith in its most naive. Even in a religious hymn which has achieved great popularity, and is to be found in all Jewish prayer books, we say: "He is Lord of the world, who reigned ere any creature yet was formed." But ere any creature yet was formed, over what did He reign? That is to say, God's royalty is not like that of the king of a country, who is not a king if he has no country over which to reign. Similarly, a man cannot be a prime minister, pure and simple – he can only be a prime minister of an existent state. If there is no state, it would be meaningless to say he is prime minister. But God's royalty is His essence and is not functional. God is king in Himself, and His kingship is in no way dependent on the existence of anything over which He reigns. Thus does Maimonides explain the Divine name *"El Shaddai"* (usually translated as God Almighty) : "That it is sufficient (*she–dai*) Himself, for He is content with His own being and requires not the being of another."

Maimonides is deeply aware of the importance of the problem of the eternity or the creation of the world, which is the problem of whether the universe is limited or unlimited in time, and which involves the conception of the essence of time itself – a problem which has occupied metaphysical – not only religious – thought ever since there was philosophy, and it is doubtful whether it could be determined by rational argument. But Maimonides does not regard its theological dimension as significant for the foundations of faith – which, according to Maimonides' view, are independent of this issue – but in its influence on the psychology of the believer. It is only for the sake of strengthening the belief in God in the minds of the majority of people, whose capacity for true faith is weak, that he gives preference to the belief in creation over the view that the world is eternal. Where reason cannot determine the issue, religious interest decides the matter.

This issue is extensively discussed in *The Guide to the Perplexed* – but in *Mishneh Torah* and in his *Commentary on the Mishnah*, Maimonides virtually disregards it. In *Yesodei ha-Torah*, Maimonides avoids the use of the terms "creator" and "creation," instead of which we read, in *Halachah* 1, the philosophical expression "and He gives being to all beings," which can be variously interpreted. Even in "The Thirteen Articles of the Creed," which are well known and included in every prayer book, and which are a simplification (in fact, an unsuccessful vulgarization) of the thirteen "fundaments" formulated by Maimonides in his introduction to his commentary on *Helek*, there is in Maimonides' original words no explicit article of faith maintaining that God created the world; here, too, the issue is circumvented by employing the formula "the cause of being of all beings, in Whom is the being of their existence and from Whom is their being." Among these thirteen "fundaments" there is one concerned with the existence of God, one concerned with His oneness, one with depriving Him of corporeality, and the like – but there is no "fundament" concerned with God as the creator of the universe. This is in accordance with Maimonides' conception, that the great principle of religious faith is to believe in God as to His being God, not as to any function ascribed to Him.

# VII.

## *Questions and Answers: Being and Creation: "The God of Aristotle and the God of Our Fathers"*

Many questions have been addressed to me regarding the matter presented in the previous chapters, their main thrust being requests for clarification of the distinction between "who gives being to all beings" and "the creator of the universe," and for an understanding of the relation between the concept of the creator–God and that of God who is to be worshipped. These questions deserve a special chapter in the attempt to throw more light on these issues.

"He gives being to all beings" – this is said of God in the first *halachah* of *Yesodei ha-Torah*. Anyone who is not familiar with the profound philosophical problems involved in concepts like "being," "a being," "to be" and the like, may simplify matters and identify "who gives being to all beings" with the "creator of all," and conceive – again, in a rather simplified manner – of "creator" as signifying a certain act of creation at a certain given moment. This is not so. First, one should realize that "to give being" (in our context) is a transitive verb, which means causing the existence of existing things, but without specifying the nature of this causation. If we apply this verb to God and the world, it means that the world exists because there is God, but nothing is said by it concerning the nature of the relation between God and the world, and whether this is a relation based on a specific act performed at a specific time. In the conception held to be a simple faith in the creation of

53

the world, the ending of the *halachah*, "..and all things in heaven or on earth or between them have no being ..." would have been completed with the words "except for the fact that God had created them." But Maimonides completes this sentence with the words "except from the truth of His being." What is said here is nothing more than that the being of all things which are not true being is conditioned on the fact that God is true being. The speculative background for the recognition of the existence of God is that the existence of all things perceived by the senses, which are not true being, involves of necessity the being of one thing (at least) which is true being. This recognition is in no way dependent on assuming that the world had some beginning in time or in rejecting such an assumption. The world exists because there is God, and the recognition of this is independent of the answer we provide to the question of whether the world has existed only from a certain time, in which God made it come out of nothing. It is even likely that the last words of the previous sentence are entirely meaningless, since we are incapable of grasping in our thought the very concepts of a beginning of time and of the world. The world is what exists, and what exists has no relation to time – but its being is no true being, it is not itself a true being. It exists because there is a true being, and that true being is God.

From the existence of things whose being is only possible and contingent and is not logically necessary – that is, things which have no true being – one has to conclude to the being of something whose being is involved in its own essence. Those things which we call beings exist because there is a cause for their being. A thing whose being is derived from the being of something else – in other words, which exists on a certain condition – is not true being. Truth is not truth on condition: it is truth in itself, and its validity is in itself; otherwise, it is not truth in the profound philosophical significance of this word. According to a philosophical deduction which we cannot analyze here in detail, a conditional being is impossible unless there is an unconditional being. This, in an extremely simplified way, is the road leading our cognition from concrete sensual reality to God, who is beyond that reality.

The *Kalam*, which arrived at its concept of the creator of the universe in a similar manner, identified this creator with the God of religious belief, whose divinity and whose worship man takes upon himself.

This is far from being self-evident. Let us assume that, from his observation of the universe and of nature, man arrives at the cognition of the existence of that being which created this universe. Does it follow, either logically or even psychologically, that man should relate to this being, the creator of the universe, in the manner in which man relates to God in the world of religious faith? A recognition of God as the creator of the universe is not sufficient to create the relation of faith and religion between man and his God, a relation which finds its expression in the fear and love of God, in the worship of God – all three of which are embodied, for Maimonides, in the fulfillment of Torah and *mitzvot*. This is why, after all those philosophical proofs of the existence of God who is the creator of the universe, Maimonides still requires the specific religious concept of "the one Lord," who alone is being and truth. Only if God is alone being and truth, is it psychologically conceivable that man should attach himself to Him, in the religious sense of man's attachment to God, since there is nothing beside Him worthy of man's attachment.

A God recognized as nothing but the creator of the universe provides man with no reason, logical or psychological, to attach himself to Him. This opens a wide avenue for the understanding of Maimonides' attitude to the issue of the worship of God.

* * *

Maimonides' contemplation and philosophical discussion of the philosophical "demonstrations" of the existence of God has no doubt aroused among some of my readers (presumably on account of what they already know from the writings of some of Maimonides' recent scholars and commentators) the feeling that Maimonides' concept of divinity is a philosophical concept, similar to that of Aristotle, whose methods of thought and analysis Maimonides employs.

55

This is a mistaken impression. It is true that Maimonides uses, in his demonstrations of the existence of God, Aristotle's method of philosophical analysis and Aristotle's categories of thought – but the God toward whom these demonstrations are directed is not the god of Aristotle, but the God of Jewish religious faith. Amongst the four philosophical demonstrations used by Maimonides, in most of which he follows Aristotle, he ascribes the greatest weight not to the recognition of God as the cause of the universe; not to regarding Him as the beginning of processes in natural reality; not to His recognition as the creator of the universe; but to recognition of Him as a being which is truth and beside which there is no truth.

Maimonides' reason for this preference is that recognition of God as the first cause, or as the beginning of the processes in nature, or as the first mover in the chain of movements, or even as the creator of the universe, is nothing more than a purely intellectual affair. It is a knowledge acquired by man, but it does not commit man to anything. On the other hand, a recognition of God as to the truth of His being – that is, that His being is true being, and beside it there is no truth and no being – has an immense emotional impact, since a man who has thought of God and conceived of Him with this kind of recognition can no longer help feeling that there is nothing else worthy of the attachment of man and of his attention except the attachment to God and "occupying oneself with God" (Maimonides' own expression, *Guide* 3:51) since every other thing, even if its importance for man's objective existence is extremely great, is meaningless and valueless. Here there is some point in repeating what we have already said: Maimonides lends a deep philosophical expression to the religious awareness which appears as pure faith, with no philosophical wrappings, in our Yom Kippur prayer – that the whole existence of man is vanity. What, then, is left for a man who has comprehended this profound truth? "From the creation did You distinguish man, and did give him knowledge how to present himself before You."

For Maimonides, the world and man are not the primary facts, for the explanation and understanding of which he knows God. Maimonides is as distant from this superficial philosophy of religion as he is from that religious naivete which presents itself in the guise of pure faith, and which, just like that philosophy of religion, requires God as the cause of the existence of the world and of man, and as a condition for the understanding of the world and of man. Popular religious philosophy as well as popular naive religion make – mainly unconsciously, but sometimes even consciously – the world and man the center and purpose, and God a mere means for the sake of the world and man. For Maimonides, on the other hand, "the Lord is God," as true being in and for Himself, *not* for being the cause of the universe, the creator of the universe, or the beginning of the processes of the universe. Hence Maimonides' proofs for the existence of God are not primarily directed toward knowledge of Him as the beginning, but toward knowledge of Him as the final purpose. As against a view which has often been aired and which is also espoused by many modern scholars, one should state categorically that Maimonides' God is the God of Abraham, Isaac and Jacob, not the god of Aristotle. True, neither is He the God of popular folk religiosity, which pretends to be pure and innocent faith, and turns God into a steward of human society, fulfilling for–its–own–sake the functions of Supreme Minister of Health, Supreme Minister of Justice, Supreme Minister of Police, Supreme Minister of Welfare, and Supreme Minister of Economic Affairs. Maimonides' God is not the bearer of some specific functions, but "The Lord is God"!

# VIII.

## *God and Man; God and Morals; God and History*

We have already indicated above that the theocentricity (God as the center) of Maimonides' conception of the world repudiates the idea of man's centrality in the creation and the view of man as the purpose of creation.

From this absolutely theocentric view of the world some conclusions follow which are hardly reconcilable with the sort of religiosity which holds itself to be pure faith. We have already mentioned some of these conclusions above, and we can add to them Maimonides' repudiation of the idea of the resurrection of the dead in the sense it has in folk religion, a sense which is expressive of the presumption of man who aspires to a rank of divinity, as it were, and demands eternity for oneself. Maimonides' discussions of this issue are sometimes obscure, concealing more than they reveal, and are sometimes expressed in language suitable to the people to whom they are addressed – as, for example, the *Epistle Concerning the Resurrection of the Dead*, if, indeed, it is authentic.* An accurate reading shows without any doubt that Maimonides reduces the concept of the resurrection of the dead to the half-mystical, half-philosophical idea of the fusion between man's acquired intellect, which is tantamount to the knowledge of God

---

* Some scholars suspect that this Epistle is a forgery, and that it was composed as a part of the great controversy about Maimonides in the generation following his death.

acquired by a man, and the active intellect – in other words, knowledge of God is what is implied by the resurrection of the dead.

We have already pointed out above the contrast between the doctrines of Maimonides and what is called "religious humanism" or "ethical monotheism," since any humanistic and moralistic world-view is of necessity anthropocentric (with man at the center). Here, some of the greatest thinkers, including a great Jew like Hermann Cohen, have been greatly mistaken when they drew parallels between Maimonides' ethic and the ethical views of Kant. For Maimonides, who recognizes only God as true being and ascribes no value or significance to man except in his knowledge of God, morality has no essential and intrinsic value, but only an instrumental significance. He regards morality as nothing but a means required by man for the purpose of making him free for his one great aim, which is knowledge of God. In the last resort, this means is only of value as far as it is useful for removing the psychological obstacles from man's way toward perfection, which is the knowledge of God. In Maimonides' thought, there is a chasm separating the sacred and the profane, the world of all human categories and values and the world of the proximity to God – and this same chasm also separates Maimonides' ethical doctrine from that of Kant. The place occupied in Kant's world by ethics as the chief element in man's essence is occupied in Maimonides' doctrine by the theory of prophecy, but an elaboration on this is beyond the scope of this work. In Kant's doctrine, the personality of every man, inasmuch as he is a man, is an end in itself and a supreme value. In Maimonides' doctrine, the perfect man is depicted as a man who is capable of withdrawing from all the occupations of this world, including the relations between himself and other persons, and of directing himself to a full preoccupation with the Holy One, blessed be He. Great religious courage is required in order to maintain that the man who fulfills the commandments is "preoccupied with Him, and not with any other." But this doctrine of Maimonides is perfect belief in the oneness of God, pure monotheism – not the ethical monotheism of nineteenth century liberalism, which also has its champions today; that ethical monotheism for which the human category of morality is the main thing, and for which God's only function is to be a guarantor of morality. Maimonides, who does not recognize material attributes of God, does not recognize moral attributes of God either. Even lovingkindness, judgement and righteousness, which are divine attributes employed by the prophets (."..the Lord who exercises lovingkindness, judgement and righteousness" – Jeremiah 9:24), are interpreted by Maimonides not as qualities to be ascribed to God, but as indications of natural reality, which is God's creation, insofar as man can grasp it and understand its laws (*Guide* 3:53).

Another weighty conclusion follows from this absolute theocentric world-view. Every human historical phenomenon and every human historical vision becomes, for Maimonides, subsidiary to religious existence and religious experience. Knowledge of past events in the history of mankind as a whole and in the history of Israel, including "miraculous" events, in which "the finger of God" was revealed, as it were – such knowledge is not the core of religious faith and is incapable of providing its foundation: "For miracles are only convincing to those who witnessed them; whilst coming generations, who know them only from the account given by others, may consider them as untrue" (*Guide* 3:50). Faith is directed toward the present, toward the worship of God, in the world as it is and in reality as it is. This task imposed on man (or on the whole of mankind) is eternal, and it does not change with the passing of time or the alterations in circumstances. From this point of view, Maimonides' world of faith is static and ahistorical, and this is one of the greatest differences between him and the spiritual world of Rabbi Judah Halevi. The same applies to his attitude to the people of Israel as a historic entity. For Maimonides, the people of Israel is no intrinsic value in itself: the specific value of this people is the task imposed on it, which is the worship of God, as embodied in the Torah. Even prophecy, in which, according to Judah Halevi, is revealed "the divine entity" which applies only to men of the seed of Abraham, Isaac and Jacob, and is peculiar to the people of Israel, is conceived by Maimonides as the highest

60

perfection which man, *qua* man, can reach by his nature.* This is why we detect in the structure of *Hilchot Yesodei ha-Torah* four chapters devoted to God, His oneness, knowledge and attachment to Him – in which Israel is not mentioned even once; two chapters on the Sanctification of the Name of God – which are addressed to Israel alone; a chapter on prophecy – in which, again, "Israel" is not mentioned; and a chapter on the Giving of the Law – which revolves wholly around the people of Israel.

All we have said about Maimonides' attitude to the historic past applies equally to the place occupied in his faith by the consciousness of the future – that is, the vision of redemption through the Messiah. If we scan all the passages in Maimonides' works in which he deals with the future redemption, and if we check carefully not only what is said in them, but also what is *not* said in them, and sense what is hinted between the lines, we shall not be able to avoid the impression that, in the deeper layers of his faith, Maimonides did not ascribe great significance to the messianic idea, and hardly felt its necessity. He does not, of course, ignore it, since it is an integral part of Jewish tradition, religion and faith. But it is quite obvious that he places it in the world of faith not–for–its–own–sake, but as being required in order to "strengthen the weak hands" and to encourage the will to accept the burden of the kingdom of heaven in the present in anticipation of its realization in the future. This is why, on the one hand, he places the belief in the coming of the Messiah among the Thirteen Articles (his "fundaments"), but on the other hand, he narrows down its significance. This is recognizable even in a youthful treatise of his, the *Epistle on Apostasy*, written to save from utter despair a Jewish community which was being troubled and oppressed, physically as well as spiritually. He underlines and emphasizes the firm Jewish belief in the certainty of redemption, but at the same time declares that our duty – and our choice as well– to worship God by fulfilling

---

* The space limitations imposed on this work prevent us from devoting a discussion to Maimonides' doctrine of prophecy, despite its central position in his religious and philosophical anthropology.

the Torah and its commandments is not dependent on it or conditioned by it, and that this duty and this choice are valid and stand even if there were no such certainty. "The duty of fulfilling the commandments is not dependent on the coming of the Messiah," he writes, "but we are in duty bound to engage in Torah and *mitzvot* and to endeavour to make their practice perfect. And once we have done what we are bound to do, if God gives us or our children's children the privilege of beholding the Messiah – how much better; but if not, we have lost nothing; on the contrary, we have gained by doing what is our duty to do." A similar tone, even if in a less explicit manner, is to be detected in the *Letter to the Jews of Yemen*. Maimonides' *Commentary on the Mishnah* is the place where the belief in the coming of the Messiah is presented as one of the "fundaments"; at the same time, it has no mention in *Yesodei Ha-Torah*, the Fundaments of the Torah. Even in *Hilchot Teshuvah*, the Laws of Repentance, which treat of the purpose of fulfilling the commandments and the boon which awaits those who fulfill them, Messianic redemption appears only once, in an answer to the question, "Why did the prophets, Sages and Righteous of Israel desire the coming of the Messiah?" The answer is that they desired and yearned for existential conditions which would fit man and nation for knowledge of God and His worship, which are alone the "good" and the "purpose." Most important of all are the last chapters of *Hilchot Melachim*, the Laws of Kings, which conclude *Mishneh Torah*, and in which Maimonides provides us with a systematic exposition of the issues of the Messiah, the redemption of Israel, and the perfection of the world in the future. To this sublime vision, he adds the following highly significant words: "But a man is never to occupy himself with *aggadot* or to spend much time on *midrashim* concerning these issues, nor to make these things central, since they lead neither to *fear of God* nor to *love of God*." Here we have reached again the two basic concepts of Maimonides' world of faith, the two central terms in his formulation of his doctrine of belief. The perfection to which faith and worship lead does not consist in what is achieved through faith and worship – not even Messianic redemption – but in faith and worship themselves – "for their own sake," as against "not for their own sake." A perfect man does not require Messianic redemption: he arrives at the purpose of man in the world as it is.

# IX.

## *Between Thought and Action: Faith and Halachah*

Toward the end of the last chapter, we evoked the two great concepts of *Fear* and *Love* of God. These are almost the last two words in Maimonides' great accomplishment, *Mishneh Torah*. On these two things, fear of God and love of God, stands the whole world of Maimonides.

At first sight, both are matters of the heart, sentiments, which do not in themselves involve any actions. Maimonides does, indeed, say this explicitly: "To the ultimate perfection of man do not belong either actions or moral qualities, but only opinions" – and the "opinions" he speaks of here are nothing but knowledge of God. This, too, has given rise to a very popular error in understanding Maimonides – as though he undervalues the acts of worship of God and reduces faith to a cognitive content alone. Nothing could be further from the truth. In speaking of "knowledge" on the one hand and of "actions and moral virtues" on the other, Maimonides makes a clear distinction between man inasmuch as he contemplates and thinks, and man inasmuch as he acts and does, and in this distinction he follows Aristotle. And again, following in the steps of Aristotle, he sees no value and purpose except in thinking and its attainments ("the depiction of concepts in the soul," in his expression), and in the knowledge of "truths in God" – which are the "opinions" mentioned. But Maimonides also knows that man is not "a separate intellect" – that is, an entity which only thinks – but an "intellect existing in

64

matter." Man is an element in natural reality, and as a natural material entity, man is consigned to action and activity within that reality. He cannot be pure thought. Hence man's great problem – what should he do? After all, by his nature he is condemned to action in the world of "acts of vanity and derangement," which are most of man's occupations, and which constitute psychological and intellectual barriers between him and his knowledge of God. What is man to do in a world in which every action is devoid of intrinsic reality and intrinsic value? What is left to man in such a world? One can only say: *in the realm of spirit* – knowledge of God to the best of his ability. But since man is not a pure intellect whose whole being is intellectual cognizance, and he also exists in the realm of action, what is left for him *in the realm of action*? One can only say: worship of God. Hence the crucial importance allotted in Maimonides' doctrine to the Torah, embodied in the *halachah*, in commandments and prescriptions, in laws and ordinances. Only such worship of God relates man to true reality, and only this is not one of the "acts of vanity and derangement on which the ignorant multitude waste all their days and strength" – fighting as they do for the satisfaction of their physical, psychological and material needs, which are purely imaginary needs.

But in order to comprehend the profound significance of the fact that the author of *The Guide to the Perplexed* is also the author of *Mishneh Torah*, we should understand the main outline of Maimonides' philosophical anthropology, of his doctrine of man, which he summed up in a semi-popular style in the first of his *Eight Chapters*. "The human soul is one," where the meaning of "soul" in this context is the whole complex of life functions in man, both those regarded as physical and those regarded a psychical, from the activities of the organs of nutrition and generation, through the senses, memory and imagination, to desires and impulses which determine a man's behavior and character – to his intellectual power. All these "faculties of the soul" are functions of one factor – the human soul. It thus appears that the concept of "the human soul" is parallel to what we today call by the name of personality. None of these activities, or powers, is a unit which can act

65

separately, since they are "parts" of the one soul, which sets them in position. A man never acts except with his whole being. In terms of Aristotelian philosophy, this soul is defined as the "form" of a man, whose "matter" is his living body.

As against this conception of personality, there is another approach, the dualistic psycho-physical one, which maintains that man is composed of two entities: a physical one – the body and its functions; and a spiritual one – the soul and its functions (and it is obvious that the meaning of the concept of "soul" is different in these two conceptions). Since they are two, it is possible for each of them to act in isolation, although in a living man they meet and are capable of interacting. This is – in a very extreme simplification – Plato's doctrine of man. There were also in ancient thought a number of pluralistic conceptions, which distinguished in man a number of "souls" – as many as the activities of man which are known to us. Among the large majority of thinkers, propounders and champions of all these conceptions – whether philosophers, moralists, or men of religion and faith – there was an agreement that the rank and the attainments of the spiritual functions were higher, in terms of value, than those of the physical functions and their attainments, sometimes to the point of regarding the latter, while necessary, as being devoid of value, and even despicable.

Maimonides knew of all these conceptions from their Greek sources – through the mediation of Arabic literature – and he opted for the view of Aristotle. Why did he do this? At first sight, the Platonic conception of the spiritual soul inhabiting the crude material body would appear to be closer to the Biblical view ("would appear to be," since there is no systematic and unambiguous clarification in the Bible of the body-soul relation) – and, in any case, it is close to the view current in the world of the Talmudic Sages, of Midrashic and Aggadic thought and of Jewish ethical and moral literature, a view which is accepted among the majority of believers. Maimonides was, of course, aware of all this, and yet he decided against the accepted "religious" view. There is no doubt that he did it out of his most profound awareness of religion and faith, as a man of the *halachah*, before whose eyes the practical commandments of Judaism were always present. The champions of psycho-physical dualism, in the various religions and systems of morality, tend to ascribe a significance of value to the activities and the attainments of the "soul" alone, and to regard the matters of the body as irrelevant from the point of view of value. This is why their doctrines revolve mostly around matters of the heart ("heart, not in its anatomical sense, but in the symbolic one), of consciousness, of intention, of belief (in the usual sense of this word). Christianity went further in this than all others, and its first appearance in history involved the abolition of the practical commandments. Maimonides, who regarded the practical commandments as a constitutive part of Judaism, rejected the separation between body and soul, and regarded man as a psycho-physical unity. In the light of this conception, it is obvious that the commandments were given *to man*, not just to *the soul of man*, and that faith – which he identifies with worship of God – cannot be restricted to knowledge and intention: it must also be the worship of God with our body.

This is how Maimonides, the man who believed in knowledge of a transcendent God, became the man of the *halachah*, whose main preoccupation was with the *magnum opus* which instructs man in his religious behavior in everyday life.

# Faith and Theology

Maimonides, the greatest believer in the world of Judaism, is also Judaism's greatest theologian. The distinction between faith and theology is obvious to a man who treats religion as an object of his study. It is not at all obvious to many people who live and experience religion. The center of any theology is its doctrine of the divine, and it is probable that this is where theology, which is thought about religion, its contents and its institutions, differs from religion itself – some would say, from faith – which is an existential reality of man from the point of view of his cognition and of his way of life. Yet it is impossible to draw a firm line between theology and the philosophy of religion, or sometimes, between theology and philosophy – and in the case of many religious people, between theology and faith. Religious faith can exist without a theology, or with a minimal theology, when the consciousness of a religious man is directed toward his standing in the presence of God rather than toward opinions or reflections concerning God. On the other hand, there is a kind of religiosity which is loaded with theology. Both types of religiosity can exist side by side within the same religion; and there have been thinkers within Judaism who regarded the *halachah* as its theology and the 613 *mitzvot* as its articles of creed.

Maimonides, although he was the greatest *halachic* authority, was not of that opinion. As the theologian, his doctrine of divinity was the foundation of his faith. When we undertake to discuss Maimonides' *faith*, we are obliged to deal with this doctrine, but we find this discussion extremely difficult precisely within the lines we have drawn. Our subject is the faith of Maimonides, not his philosophy; yet in his theology, faith and philosophy are inextricably intertwined. In the philosophy of religion – and Maimonides himself was *not* a philosopher of religion! – Maimonides' theology is sometimes defined as a "negative theology," since in its essence it consists of the negation of the divine attributes current in human religious discourse, in which God – "the one," the "true being" – is conceived, as it were, in categories of human thought derived from the sensual or imaginative experience of man. Let us attempt to deal with this profound issue on the basis of the simplified and popular formulation given to it in the Thirteen Articles of the Creed in our prayer book: "That the Holy one, blessed be his name, is not a body, and He cannot be perceived by the perceptions of the body" (i.e, by concepts borrowed from the cognizance and experience of man, flesh and blood), "And He has no resemblance whatsoever."

Anyone who has comprehended the full significance of these three negations must ask himself whether Maimonides was a theist. In the philosophy of religion, one tends to define as theism the belief in a "God who is a person" (a "personal God"), as distinct from a god who is an abstract concept; and it is the general view that a God who is a person is the God of religious belief, whereas a god who is an abstract concept belongs in the world of non-religious philosophical thought, and a belief in such a god is virtually a-theism. In the light of this distinction, the question has been raised: If the Holy one, Blessed be His name, is, according to Maimonides, not a body; not perceived by the perceptions of the body, and has no resemblance whatsoever, does Maimonides' God still have the character of a person? What could be the religious significance of a belief in such a God? It could be maintained that such questions – if we were to discuss them in the categories of speculative theology – are semantic questions rather than religious questions, questions which are concerned merely with the meanings of concepts. But there is a possible approach to such questions also from the side of living religiosity. In this case, the question of theism becomes: Was Maimonides' faith a religious faith?

There is no doubt that an entity conceived as devoid of all attributes which could be ascribed to it is no "person" in any of the senses of this word in the categories of man's thinking about the reality known to him. But if we free ourselves from burrowing into the semantics of "person" and "theism" and turn to religion as a living reality, we can reach a definition of theism as religious belief, not from the point of view of formal logic, but from an "operational" point of view, as to its embodiment in human reality. We are then allowed, or even bound, to define as theism not the belief in a "personal God" or in a "divine personality," but a belief which recognizes *that there is God, and that He can be worshipped.* Here we have the difference between Maimonides' God and Aristotle's or Spinoza's god. These three men were all thinkers who applied philosophical thought to the concept of divinity. Maimonides liked to quote the words of King David to his son Solomon: "Know you the God of your father, and serve Him" (I Chron. 28:9). All three thinkers would be at one as to the demand to know God – but would differ as to their conclusions. Whereas the god of Aristotle and the god of Spinoza are gods to which the very concept of worship is inapplicable and would become meaningless if applied to them, the God of Maimonides is precisely that entity whom, and whom alone, one should worship. In this respect, the whole of Maimonides' faith is epitomized in the whole of this maxim: "Know you the God of your father, and serve Him."

This is the purest and the most proper theism – the supreme expression given by Maimonides to the Jewish perception of God, a perception embodied in the Torah and its commandments.

# XI.

## *Choice and Providence I*

If this pure theism, the monotheism of the Jewish faith, is recognition of the *one* God – the significance of whose oneness and uniqueness is that He is not to be described by attributes derived from human experience and imagination, and therefore man cannot imagine Him – is there any relation between God and man? The answer has already been given: there is a relation, and it consists in faith. But so far we have only been acquainted with the faith in God in a negative fashion – that one should not believe in anything other than God. This in itself is no small matter, and we have seen that one of the Talmudic Sages said that whoever repudiates idolatry is called a Jew – but this is not yet to say that he has become a Jew through this repudiation alone. One should still ask: What is the positive content of faith which forms the spiritual and psychological image of a Jew – who is, in Maimonides' view, one who believes in a transcendent God, in a God who is beyond the sensual and imaginative cognition of man? What is the content which is, for Maimonides, the contact between God and man? This contact is man's awareness of the *divine providence*.

The doctrine of divine providence is one of the greatest chapters in Maimonides' whole teaching, and it reflects his religious faith in a far clearer manner than his philosophical demonstrations of the existence of God, which he himself considered as his main achievement. The discussion of providence is intertwined, for Maimonides, with the discussion of the problem of God's knowledge – God's knowledge of the world, of man and his actions, and

even of his thoughts and desires. These concepts of divine providence and knowledge raise, within the world of faith, the crucial
question: what is the position of man in the world, if he is
supervised by God, who knows and is aware of him? What are the
possibilities open before man in his world? What is his potential for
action? What can be required of him, and is to be required of him
in practice? This is the point of confrontation between the concepts
of divine knowledge and providence on the one hand, and human
free choice on the other hand.

Maimonides discusses these issues in all his great works, in his
*Commentary on the Mishnah* as well as in *Mishneh Torah*, *The
Guide to the Perplexed*, and his responsa to people who asked him
questions on this problem. Out of all these discussions, one can
piece together a large panorama of Maimonides' view of divine
providence. Its starting point is a discussion of the famous maxim
of Rabbi Akiva in *Avot* 3:19 – a short maxim of four words in the
Hebrew original: "Everything is foreseen, yet freedom of choice is
given." On this maxim, Maimonides remarks: "This saying includes very momentous issues, and it is worthy of Rabbi Akiva."

The contemplation of this concentrated maxim of Rabbi Akiva
leads us to immense problems, both problems of faith and of
philosophical thought, of ethics, of the doctrine of values and of
man's self-understanding. What is embedded in these words are the
concepts of providence and of divine decree in religious thought; of
causality and possibility in the philosophical doctrine of being; of
duty and potential in ethics; and of responsibility and punishment
in jurisprudence. Maimonides immediately points out the problems
involved in these four words of Rabbi Akiva: "This is its meaning,
but briefly: everything that is in the world is known to Him, blessed
be His name, and conceived by Him. But you are not to think that
since He knows all actions, it would follow that man is forced in his
actions to perform any particular act. This is not the case, but man
has permission to do what he would do." This explains the maxim
in its literal sense, but it does not explain its meaning, since these
words appear to contain the most glaring contradiction.   God's
knowledge – if the knowledge spoken of here has a meaning in

human terms – is obviously true. It follows that the future is predetermined – but how, then, is it possible for man to do good or evil? And again – if we continue to use categories of human thought – how could a man be accountable for a certain act, or be held responsible for a deed he has done, if this deed has been permanently fixed since time immemorial in the consciousness of the Holy One, which is certainly true? This argument is aired not only by ordinary people, but also by men of thought, who take it to be an axiom that a moral or religious duty must be within the ability of man to perform; for otherwise, it would be meaningless. This is the argument that every "ought" involves "can." But this dogmatic and simplified assertion requires a considerable amount of investigation, and one can differ with it: Perhaps a moral or religious command could have significance even if one were incapable of performing it? We see immediately that the problem of divine knowledge and human choice is interconnected with the problems of divine providence and of the justice of divine reward and punishment, which are held to be among the foundations of religious faith. One should also note that, even apart from the problem of divine knowledge and from the factors of religious faith, there is a crucial philosophical and ethical problem, parallel to the problem of religion and faith, as long as one thinks in terms of causality. From the point of view of such concepts, the same problem of knowledge and choice exists, even if we have no subject of that knowledge that we know of. For, as to the certainty and necessity of what is to happen in the future, it makes no difference whether there is a knowledge embedded in the subjective consciousness of someone who has true knowledge, or if there is a knowledge embedded in the objective information enclosed in the causal chain of the evolution of things one from the other according to the necessary laws of reality. If we then identify man's moral decisions with his choice between the various possibilities, where is the choice here?

Maimonides presents the problem of determinism as against free choice as a religious and moral problem; as the confrontation between belief in God's knowledge and placing on man the responsibility for his decisions and his actions. In order to understand Maimonides' position and its place in the world of Jewish faith, one should correct the error inherent in the current view which maintains that religious faith involves of necessity a belief in free choice. Even from our empirical data – the history of religious thought, of religious beliefs and opinions – we learn that religious faith is in no way conditioned on a definite answer to this question. We know various forms of very profound religious faith which are based precisely on belief in predestination. Even in Judaism itself, opinions vary to a very large extent, and even in the Bible – where there is no systematic theological discourse – one can find passages which seem to support both points of view. It is very easy to point out those outstanding verses of the Torah which assert that man has before him "good and evil, life and death," and which require him to choose good, or "life" – as well as the many passages of the prophets calling on man to repent. But the advocates of the literal meaning of the texts must not forget that in all these places, man is *required* to choose, without any mention of a guarantee *that he is able to choose*; and that there are verses which can be interpreted to mean that man's actions, or even his intentions, are directed and guided from above. The same applies to the words of the Talmudic Sages in all our Talmudic sources, *halachah* as well as *aggadah*. In the world of philosophizing religious thought within Judaism, we have the contrast between Maimonides, who presents the image of man in his human freedom as an objective fact, and Maimonides' stringent critic, Rabbi Hasdai Crescas, who is also one of the greatest figures in Jewish faith and religious thought, and who restricts man's freedom to his subjective consciousness, and makes it subservient to the general chain of cause and effect in God's creation. But both Maimonides, who appears to be an extreme indeterminist, and Crescas, who is very close to determinism, were perfectly good Jews as far as the acceptance of the burden of the kingdom of heaven and of Torah and *mitzvot* is concerned.

# XII.

## *Choice and Providence II*

The theological task which Maimonides took upon himself on this issue of divine providence and human choice was to maintain man's free choice in a world which God created in accordance with His will (to use the language of the *Kaddish*), and which He conducts according to the regularity which He implanted in it. But how can one combine free choice with such cosmic determinism, which is the will of God?

In the popular conception of the belief in divine providence, as well as in its reflections in the literature of religious thought, there is a popular distinction between general providence and special providence. The simplistic sense in which these concepts are comprehended is that God is attributed with the functions of pulling the strings of the universe, administering the business of creation, and looking after the interest of His creatures. This is a belief in a functional God, a belief in a God for the sake of the world, and especially for the needs and requirements of man. This is anthropocentric religiosity which leads to the worship of God "not–for–its–own–sake." What is more, it is doubtful whether one could reconcile these concepts of the two kinds of providence with each other. Maimonides, led by the strength of his belief in God in His Godhead rather than from the point of view of the interests and needs of creation of His creatures, elevates these two concepts of providence to the highest level, that directed toward God and not toward man. He makes these two concepts of general and special providence refer to two different levels of reality, and by doing this, he avoids any contradiction between them.

The significance of general providence is found by Maimonides to be explicitly expressed in the words of the Prophet Jeremiah (9:24): "...that I am the Lord, who exercises unfailing love, justice and righteousness in the earth." On the face of it, unfailing love, justice and righteousness are categories of human consciousness, intention and action, and in this human sense it is impossible to ascribe them to God. But for Maimonides they reflect reality as it exists by the will of its creator. God's *unfailing love* is nothing but the existence of the created world. God's *justice* is the causal relation imprinted by the creator into the relations between the constituents of His creation, and from which follows the regular evolution of all things in the world from one another. In other words, the determination which reigns in nature is itself God's judgement. God's *righteousness* is the potential accorded by the creator to living creatures to act spontaneously, of their own accord, unlike the inorganic world, the constituents of which are passive and are only put in action by the causality imprinted on the world (*Guide* 3:53). To this general providence, mankind is of course also subject, since it is part of natural reality, and so is every single human being as an individual, inasmuch as his existence is part of the order of the world of nature as it was determined by its creator. But out of this regularity, by a special dispensation of the creator, man's will was disengaged, and he was given, from this point of view, independence – or "permission," in the words of Rabbi Akiva. This is the meaning of the great proclamation of Maimonides: "May the Master of the will be praised, whose design and wisdom cannot be fathomed!" (*Guide* 1:2)   What, then, is left of the idea of special providence, which has been so deeply ingrained in religious consciousness? On the face of it, the whole Bible testifies to this sort of providence, both the Torah and the Prophets, and this has been a foundation of faith for the sages and thinkers of all generations in Judaism. How can this be reconciled with general providence, to which man is as much subject as all the other constituents of natural reality?

Not only does Maimonides not ignore this great article of faith of special providence which is found in our religious tradition – and, needless to say, he does not abolish it – but he even elevates it to the highest level of religious faith by deepening our understanding of its true meaning (*Guide* 3:51–53). It is true that by so doing Maimonides performs something like a Copernican revolution in the interpretation of this concept.

He cannot accept the concept of special providence in the sense it has in folk religion, and in the spirit of maxims from the *midrashim* – as, for example, "A man does not lift a finger below unless it has been decreed from above"; or, "Forty days before the birth of an infant, an echo (*bat-kol*) comes out and proclaims: 'The daughter of so-and-so is to marry the son of so-and-so'" ("Marriages are made in heaven"); or the *midrashic* exegesis on Deuteronomy 22:8, "… that you do not bring blood upon your house, if any man fall from it": "If any man falls, he has been destined to fall from the first days of creation." To Maimonides, it is perfectly clear that every man, inasmuch as he is part of natural reality, is subject to the causality inherent in this natural reality and to its consequences. From this point of view, all the events of his life are included in the chain of causes and effects imprinted by the creator on His world. But man's voluntary decisions are not derived from this general reality; they are given into the hand of each individual. The most important of these decisions in Maimonides' view is the decision whether to direct man's consciousness to knowledge of God and His worship or to direct it toward any other purpose.

The decision "to occupy oneself with Him, blessed be His name, and not with the affairs of the world" (in Maimonides' own sharp and bold formulation) is not implanted in the nature of the human race in general, but each individual human being is capable of accepting this decision or rejecting it. An individual who has accepted it has released himself from the world of general providence, the world of natural reality which is indifferent to any value, and has put himself in the presence of God. The standing of such a man, who has decided in favor of knowledge of God and worship of God, is what, in Maimonides' view, popular religious discourse calls by the name of special providence. In other words: the knowledge a man has of God is itself the knowledge God has of him and His providence over him. This culmination of faith for–its–own–sake is expressed by Maimonides in the following words: "Just as we perceive God by means of the light which He sends down upon us, wherefore the Psalmist says, 'In Your light shall we see light' (Ps. 36:9); so God looks down upon us through this same light, and is always with us beholding and watching us..." (*Guide* 3:52). And Maimonides adds: "Note this particularly."*

Thus, the individual is not under special divine providence by virtue of his own nature as a human being. It is incumbent on him to acquire such attachment for himself, and this providence is embodied in his attachment to God, which also includes what is called the survival of the soul. He who has attained this rank "is with his God, and his God is with him." His existence is turned from an indifferent natural event to a significant fact, which includes the survival of his soul. Within the limits we have put upon ourselves in these chapters, we have no place here to clarify Maimonides' theory of the soul and the concept of its survival in his doctrine. Suffice it to underline here that his conception of the survival of the soul is part and parcel of that knowledge of God which is in man, and which is itself eternity. Anyone who has not reached this rank remains part of natural reality; he remains under the governance of universal providence alone – that is, he is subject to the rule of what appears to men as meaningless accident.

Thus we have solved the problem of how to reconcile the concept of universal, or general, providence with that of special providence. Universal providence is the way of the world, implanted in it by its creator, and we comprehend it as the system of the laws of nature. Special providence is not something accorded to a man from above; it is an attainment arrived at by man if he directs himself toward God. He is favored with God's providence

---

* One should note that in all those places in *The Guide to the Perplexed* where Maimonides ends a passage with the words "and note this"; "and note"; "and note this particularly" and the like, he is pointing out some innovation of his.

78

inasmuch as he is attached to God in the knowledge he has of Him.

Like all the contents of religious consciousness, the belief in providence is also not the same for all believers. Maimonides explains time and again that it has two different levels: one, for those capable of the worship of God for–its–own–sake, and the other, for those who worship God not for His own sake. The latter are incapable of reaching the rank of our Father Abraham, "to worship out of love." But the Torah has made it *permissible* for men "to worship God and to fulfill the commandments in the hope of reward and abstain from the prohibitions for fear of punishment," and those who do so are also recognized as worshippers of God. Only those who perform the worship of God for His own sake, however, are the perfect worshippers. Maimonides emphasizes again and again that these constitute a minority, and that those who worship "not–for–its–own–sake" are the large majority. They are not ruled out of the community of the worshippers of God, since in practice they do worship God – but they have not reached perfection. According to the comprehension of the "crowd of believers" – an expression often used by Maimonides – God's supervision over them is like the supervision of a shepherd over his flock, or a driver's supervision over the movements of his car, or the supervision by the police of the order of society – in all of which the supervisor is charged with the needs of those under his supervision. He who believes in God *in truth* identifies God's providence over him with the degree of his own proximity to God. He recognizes that God is with him, since he is with God. These two things are identical; they are not two different things.

Maimonides takes the two sections of the *Shema* as embodying these two human attitudes to divine providence (*Guide* 3:27–28). In the first of these sections, there is, at first sight, no indication of divine providence; it merely presents us with the categorical imperative of loving God. But it is precisely in "You shall love God" that the quintessence of providence is concentrated – a providence which is man's relation to God, not just God's relation to man. The second section presents providence from the point of view of God's relation to man. The commandments for the worship of God are supported by utilitarian arguments and fortified by warnings. Maimonides ascribes to this presentation only an educational value. But the profound distinction which he draws between these two conceptions of providence is expressed in his interpretation of the Book of Job (*Guide* 3:23).

Job's bold recrimination against God's governing of the world originated in an erroneous conception of divine providence, which he derived from views current among the common believers. "I have heard of You by the hearing of the ear" (Job 42:5). From the point of view of this conception, Job regarded his fate as an act of divine negligence – the divine policeman had not fulfilled His task. But once he was favored with a revelation of God, Job recognized his mistake, and this is the second half of the same verse: "...but now my eye sees You." Maimonides emphasizes that this revelation was a description of "natural objects, and nothing else; it describes the elements, meteorological phenomena, and peculiarities of various kinds of living beings." Job reaches the profound recognition that we cannot "compare the manner in which God rules and manages His creatures with the manner in which we rule and manage certain beings;" the concept of divine providence is different from the concept of the policeman supervising traffic on the highway, and the concept of divine management of the world is different from that of the management of the country by a prime minister.

> The term "rule" has not the same definition in both cases; it signifies different notions, which have nothing in common but the name. In the same manner, while there is a difference between works of nature and productions of human handicraft, so there is a difference between God's rule, providence and intention in reference to all natural forces, and our rule, providence and intention in reference to things which are the objects of our rule, providence and intention. (*Guide* 3:23).

80

To sum up: the events in this world, including the events in the life of man, reflect universal, or general providence, the regularity of which the creator imprinted on His world. A man cannot expect that those events of his life which follow the chain of cause and effect of which he is part should change on account of his attainments. But each man has permission to rise above this reality by his attachment to God. The man who has reached this state by means of his will and intellect is the man called by Maimonides variously "perfect," "learned" or "pious."

The perfect man worships God because he has attained a knowledge of God without any relation to the events which befall him, just as they befall every other man. This, according to Maimonides, is the rank attained by Abraham in the act on Mount Moriah, and by Job after the revelation of God. The principle of supreme faith propounded by Maimonides – a principle which those of small faith who call themselves innocent believers find hard to comprehend – is that a man's standing before God is nothing but his own comprehension of God and such a man's worship of God. It has nothing to do with what is accorded to a man by God.

All of man's actions, including his sentiments and his behavior, are not worthy of being counted as his own deeds unless they originate from him alone, as distinct from any sentiment or behavior which comes about on account of factors which act on him, and from any act performed by him on account of such factors. This is why Maimonides, in his profound investigation of the apparent contradiction between God's knowledge and man's choice, takes a firm and unambiguous stand in favor of free choice. This applies not only to what takes place within a man's soul – what the Talmudic Sages called "fear of God" – but also to the actions a man performs of his own free will, since such actions are inseparable from the fear of God.

This conception involves a denial of the existence of such traits of character in man which exist in him by nature and over which he has no control. According to Maimonides, man himself forms his own character of his own free will. One should point out that on

this issue we can detect a certain development in Maimonides'
view. In his early *Eight Chapters* (Ch. 8), man's soul is presented as
a clean slate as to its actual characteristics. It is no more than a
complex of *potentialities*, the actualization of which and the direction of which to a certain end through the proper employment of
them is an act of man's will. It follows that, to start with, a man is
never to be defined by his character. All his "opinions"'' (i.e., the
qualities of his soul) are acquired by man himself through his
voluntary decisions, and they do not follow from what a man was to
begin with. In natural cosmic reality, Maimonides discerns the rule
of determinism*, which necessitates the evolution of every single
thing from its cause. Thus there is in nature only one distinction –
the distinction between that which is necessary being and that
whose being is impossible. But with regard to the human soul,
there is also *possible* being: the natural data of the personality
enable us to form different human characters, according to the will
of the owner of that personality. True, Maimonides admits that,
before this formation of the personality by man's self-education, by
his studies and voluntary endeavors, when his soul is still in a state
of potentiality, it is possible that this development may be somewhat influenced by a certain "preparation" for some particular
traits as against other traits; it is possible that a man has a natural
tendency toward some characteristics, a tendency which would
facilitate the acquisition of these characteristics, as against other
characteristics which would cost him much effort to acquire. This
preparation is related by Maimonides to physiology, in accordance
with the doctrine of humors of Galen's medical theory. But
Maimonides does not see in this a diminution of the principle of
free will. He states firmly that, in any case, a great effort is
required of man in order to bring into actuality even what he is
prepared for by his own nature, just as it is not impossible for him
to acquire by the effort of his will such characteristics as he is not
prepared for by nature. It follows that man himself is always

---

* Determinism in Aristotelian science is based on the concept of final causality, as
against modern science, whose determinism is based on efficient causality.

responsible for the final formation of his personality, and that he has no right to blame it on what he may describe as his "nature."

In *Hilchot Deot* in *Mishneh Torah*, we detect a slight retreat from this extreme indeterminism. Here, Maimonides adds to these two kinds of characteristics also "such characteristics which exist in a man from his conception according to the nature of his body." Although Maimonides does not treat this kind of characteristic in detail, it appears that he regards them as things which are not subject to a man's free choice. Yet he repeats, in *Hilchot Teshuvah* in the same book of *Mishneh Torah* (*Sefer ha-Mada*), the firm statement that "permission is given to every man... that he, of his own accord, in his behavior and thought, should know good and evil, and do whatever he wishes to do, and there is nothing to stop him from doing good or evil." In his words, "and there is nothing to stop him," Maimonides includes God – as against the apparent meaning of Biblical verses like "...for I have hardened his heart" (Ex. 10:1), or "...for I also withheld you from sinning against Me" (Gen. 20:6) – verses explained by Maimonides in a different fashion.

Maimonides' method of reconciling what appears to be a contradiction between the belief in divine providence and the idea of free choice is extremely audacious. Only the most profound religious faith makes it possible for a man to accept such a view. From the point of view of a deterministic philosophy which is outside the boundaries of religious faith – and Maimonides, after all, is supposed to have accepted the deterministic philosophy of Aristotle – there exists a very great intellectual difficulty in the assumption that man's voluntary decision can be released from the reign of universal causality. In philosophical ethics, this view is known as compatibilism – the view that free will is compatible with causality. Maimonides attempts to reach a solution to this problem on the basis of religious faith.

# XIII.

## *Choice and Providence III*

Maimonides is a determinist with regard to the whole of natural reality, to the concrete facts which take place in the world, since the regularity implanted in them – causality – is the will of its creator and upholder. This reality also includes the fate of man inasmuch as his objective existence as an individual is part of the complex of nature. But Maimonides is an extreme indeterminist as to the subjective existential constituents of man – his voluntary decisions. How do these two positions become reconciled with each other? The reconciliation between them is a vast intellectual accomplishment of religious faith.

The principle of man's choice is clearly and sharply formulated by Maimonides in *Hilchot Teshuvah*: "Permission is given to each man: if he wishes to direct himself to the way of good and to become righteous, it is in his hands: but if he wishes to direct himself to the way of evil and become wicked, it is also in his hands. For he himself, of his own accord and of his own knowledge and design, knows good and evil and does whatever he desires to do, and there is no one to stop him from doing good or doing evil."

But one should immediately pay considerable attention to another fact. Maimonides, who turns this principle into a cornerstone for the educational and psychological preparation of man for accepting the commandments of the Torah, does not make it an article of faith. In the Thirteen Articles of Faith, we find included the belief that God knows the actions of man and does not ignore them – and His knowledge, of course, is not a knowledge in time:

past, present and future are simultaneously open to Him. How, then, is it possible that a man, of his own accord and knowledge and design, should know good and evil and do whatever he wishes, without any one stopping him from doing good or evil? In the Thirteen Articles we find as one of the articles the belief that God rewards and punishes. It is true that each of these Articles needs a special interpretation – but at least, each of them is written. But as to man's free choice, we find no single Article of Faith. This means that the business of religious faith is nothing but man's awareness of his standing before God and the duties incumbent upon him because of his standing before God. In other words, faith is embodied in accepting the yoke of Torah and *mitzvot*. As to man's opinions concerning himself, his potentialities, his powers and his destiny – and the problem of free choice is one of them – these in no way belong to the domain of faith, although for the "innocent" believers, or those who pretend to innocence, whose aim is not for the sake of God but for their own sake, this is the core of religious faith. For Maimonides, these are metaphysical (anthropological-philosophical) problems, as to which legitimate controversies within legitimate religious faith are possible.

Three times in his *Commentary on the Mishnah*, Maimonides establishes a general rule for dealing with controversies on matters of beliefs and opinions which arise among those believing in God's Torah: "Wherever there is a controversy among Sages on an opinion concerning belief, the aim of which is not a certain action, one does not rule in such a case that the *halachah* is in accordance with one or the other" (on *Sotah* 3:5); "Any controversy which arises among Sages which does not end in action, but is a matter of a certain belief alone – one takes no side in determining that *halachah* is according to one of them" (on *Sanhedrin* 10:3); "Any opinion whatsoever which does not lead to a certain action, one does not say concerning it that the *halachah* is according to this or that side" (on *Shavuot* 1). But one should not imagine for a moment that Maimonides is "tolerant" or "liberal" in matters of *halachah*. He is one of the hardest and most strict among the *halachic* authorities on any matter of determining a practical *halachah*, and he zealously guards the truths of faith to the point of hating those who deny them, and demanding strict measures against them. But in what matters of faith? In such beliefs on which, in his view, hangs a man's readiness to take upon himself the commandments for the worship of God – such as the belief in the unity of God and the denial of corporeality to Him. A rejection of such beliefs leads of necessity to idolatry, just as the rejection of the divine origin of the Torah, or of the authority of the Oral Torah, leads to the abolition of commandments. For pragmatic – one could almost say, opportunistic – reasons, he establishes as articles of faith even such things which we know he does not regard as "true" opinions but merely as "necessary" ones – that is, opinions which may lead a man of "the crowd" to the fulfillment of the commandments, or at least strengthen him in their fulfillment. Quite different is his attitude to beliefs and opinions – even if he regards them as "true" – which are no more than "suppositions" on which man's readiness to fulfill the commandments does not depend (at least, according to Maimonides' own philosophical and psychological understanding of these matters). In this, he is revealed as a true representative of the *halachah*. One can quote in this context his words in *Sefer ha-Mitzvot*, Prohib. 47: "We should not follow our hearts until we come to believe opinions contrary to the opinions incumbent on us by the Torah; but we should confine our thoughts and put a limit to them and stop at that limit – and the limit is *the Torah's commandments and warnings*.

It is apparent that his opinion as to free choice, which is expressed in an unambiguous and absolute manner, belongs to this third kind of belief. But how is the principle of free choice – that there is nothing to stop man from choosing good or evil and doing whatever he wishes – to be reconciled with the principle that everything is known from time immemorial to God, who administers the universe and man?

In religious thought, many attempts have been made to save the idea of man's free choice without contradicting the belief in God's omniscience by separating man's decisions and actions into two levels:

a. On the one hand, man's psychological motives for certain actions lie in his own objective reality, in relation to which he feels himself, and appears to others, to be the determining factor; while in fact, his decisions and determinations are imposed on him by a superior power, called "fate" in mythical thought, "causality" in philosophical thought, and, in the world of religious belief, "special providence." On the face of it, a man does what he wishes: he chooses for himself a certain way of life, a wife, a profession, and he does not know that all this has been ordained for him.

b. On the other hand, there is a world of man's own decisions as to his subjective existence, decisions which take place in his consciousness alone, beliefs and opinions, ambitions and directions which exist deep in his heart and originate from him alone; and in regard to such things he is free.

At attempt to formulate such a distinction is a very famous maxim of our Talmudic Sages; "Everything is in the hand of God apart from the fear of God." "Everything" here means man's objective existence, including the kind of things we have just mentioned: the profession he has chosen, the place he has decided to live in, the wife he has elected to share his life. His choice of all these things had already been predetermined by God's knowledge, a knowledge which is identical with reality. An exception to this rule is man's decision to accept or not to accept the yoke of the kingdom of heaven. This decision was left by God to man.

The beginning of Maimonides' discussion of this problem is a rejection of this attempted division. To begin with, he even intensifies the difficulty. He rejects the attempt to bring about a harmony between God's knowledge and man's choice by means of taking man's actions in his objective reality out of the domain of his free voluntary decision in the subjective domain. He does not accept this easy solution because of its artificiality – one might almost term it insincerity. Even without much psychological examination and philosophical analysis, we know that the separation between the two domains which are called in a somewhat poetic language body and soul, is unrealistic and even impossible – and Maimonides does not accept this separation. We have already mentioned his assertion that "the human soul is one," where the term "soul" is employed by him to include the physical as well as the psychical functions of man. Man's psychic and spiritual reality is not separated from his natural, or even from his social, existence; and it is impossible to ascribe to him freedom to decide in one domain if he is subject to external decree (be it "fate," "causality" or "providence") as to his activities and behavior in the other domain. A man cannot be free as to his spiritual and psychical decisions and responsible for them, if he is not free as to his practical decisions and responsible for them – and therefore also for their consequences, that is, for his destiny in life.

Maimonides explains this great issue in a simple, almost popular manner in his responsum to Rabbi Obadiah the Convert. This man is an interesting case of a non-Jew who accepted Judaism, studied it and the Torah thoroughly, and reached the level of corresponding with Maimonides on matters of belief and Torah. Maimonides answers Rabbi Obadiah the Convert, who had asked him for the meaning of the Talmudic maxim "Everything is in the hand of God except fear of God," in the following words: "And what you have said, that all the deeds of men are not decreed by the creator, blessed be He, is the impeccable truth; for *all actions of men are included in the fear of God*, since the consequence of each and any action of man leads to a fulfillment of a commandment or to a transgression against a commandment. And what our Sages meant by "everything is in the hand of God" was the way of the world and its objects and its nature, such as all kinds of trees and animals and souls and metals and spheres and angels – all this is in the hands of God."

According to these words, "everything" mentioned in that Talmudic maxim is not the events in the life of man, but the natural reality in which a man is embedded; whereas the way which a man walks in his life is something he is responsible for, and the consequences of it come to him from this way of life itself and not from heaven. A man has no right to devolve responsibility for events which follow his own actions on a factor outside himself: if he thinks in mythical terms – on fate; if he thinks philosophically –

on causality; and if he thinks in religious terms – on special providence. Man himself is responsible for his way of life and for all the events in his life which are consequent upon it – not merely for the psychical content called "fear of God." But how is it possible for man to be responsible for his way of life while he is embedded in that world ("all kinds of trees and animals and souls and metals and spheres and angels") which is in the hand of God, and he himself is part of the world, subject to the causality according to which the world behaves?

Maimonides does not attempt to mitigate this problem: he presents it in the sharpest outline, but at the same time he paves a way to its solution. This solution is already hinted at in his commentary on the Mishnaic tractate *Avot*, in reference to a maxim which is not philosophical (or perhaps one should say that precisely in its simplicity is profoundly philosophical), the saying of Rabbi Elazar ha-Kappar in 4:29: "... for perforce you were created, and perforce you were born, and you live perforce, and perforce you will die, and perforce you will in the future have to give account and reckoning before the Supreme King of Kings, the Holy One, blessed be He." At first sight, this maxim contains a categorical denial of any freedom in human reality. One can understand it to imply that all events in man's life are decreed from heaven, and he is thus devoid of all choice. But Maimonides explains: "and consider his saying that perforce you are born and what follows it: perforce you live, perforce you die – all this is in reference to natural affairs, in which man has no choice, and of which our Sages have said that everything is in the hands of God except the fear of God. But the Sages did not say: perforce you sin, perforce you pass or stand or walk or sit or the like of this – for these are all affairs which are in the control of man, and there is no necessity in them." It appears thus that Maimonides does not recognize the artificial division between fear of God and man's actions. His words, that the maxim does not say" perforce you sin" agree with our Sages' maxim about the fear of God which is not in the hand of God. But he adds with emphasis that the maxim does not say "perforce you walk or sit or stand." That is: all your activities, and therefore also their consequences, are not decreed from heaven.

Man is by his nature part of natural reality; but man's voluntary activity is presented by Maimonides as an antithesis to nature. He distinguishes between the events in a man's life, which originate in his being part of natural reality and subject to its laws, which are universal providence, and man's actions, which originate in his free will. Man's ability to act of his own accord and not by necessity of his nature, and to bring about in this manner even consequences which were not embedded in reality from the beginning – this, for Maimonides, is the greatest of the wonders of creation. This potential given to man, and not those natural phenomena which arouse the wonder of the common people – is miraculous. The miracle is that man can be free of his subjection to nature, and this is a revelation of the hand of God in natural reality: "just as the Holy one, blessed be His name, wanted man to be erect, broad-chested, and have fingers [i.e., man's nature, over which he has no control] – in the same way He wanted him to move and rest *of his own accord* and perform actions *of his own choice*, without anyone forcing them on him or preventing him" (*Eight Chapters*, 8); "Just as the creator wanted fire and wind to move upwards and water and earth to move downwards, and the sphere to move in a circular motion, and the other creatures of the world to behave as it [i.e., nature] wishes – thus He wanted man to have his domain in his own hand, and all his actions to be delivered to him, and that there would be no one to force or draw him; but he, *of his own accord and of his own knowledge* given him by God, should do all that man is capable of doing" (*Hilchot Teshuvah* 5:4).

If we understand this conception of providence in Maimonides' doctrine, we shall also understand the astonishing ending of a very important chapter in *The Guide to the Perplexed*, which has caused surprise to many people. The second chapter of Part I of the *Guide* presents the significance of the story of the Garden of Eden: Adam and Eve in the Garden; the Tree of Life and the Tree of Know-ledge; the Serpent; the sin as a consequence of which Adam was driven out of the Garden of Eden. Maimonides does not regard this as the story of an event which happened at a certain time in a certain place, but as a presentation of human reality in every time and place. The man depicted in this story is not a certain individual, "the first man," but he is every man. Man, created in the image of God, was destined to live in that Garden, in which there is the Tree of Life, which is intellectual knowledge of the truth, and also the Tree of Knowledge of Good and Evil, which is the distinction which man can make, if he chooses to make it, through his imaginative faculty; between what he imagines to himself to be "good" – that is, that which he is attracted to – and that which he imagines to himself to be "evil" – that is, that which he rejects. Man was destined for cognizance of the truth, and he failed, not in distinguishing between truth and falsity, but in distinguishing between what he desires and what he rejects – "good" and "evil." Maimonides presents the whole story of the Garden of Eden as a symbol of the potential given to man to follow voluntarily "his imaginary desires." This, for him, is the meaning of the verse "And... the woman saw that the tree was *good* for food, and that it was *pleasant* to the eyes, and a tree to be *desired* to make one wise" (Genesis 3:6). Man is capable of going this way despite the image of God, which is his intellectual faculty implanted in him by God. In other words: man can behave contrary to his destiny.

The ending of this magnificent chapter is very strange – as if an exclamation has burst out of Maimonides' mouth: "May the Master of the will be praised, whose design and wisdom cannot be fathomed!" (*Guide* 1:2). The epithet "Master of the will" as applied to God is bizarre. It is not current in religious literature or in ordinary religious discourse. We remember among epithets ascribed to God in everyday language "Master of wisdom," "Master of power," "Master of bravery" and the like – but what has "Master of the will" to do here, and why does this arouse Maimonides into special wonderment? Maimonides regards as the most wondrous thing in the whole of reality the fact that God has established the world on the basis of a causal regularity implanted in it, and there was no logical reason, on the face of it, why man, who is part of this world, should have free choice; whereas the story of the Garden of Eden presents before us the miracle that man can activate his will against what has been implanted in man. *Causal regularity* implanted in the world by the creator can be conceived of by man's intellectual faculty; but "may the Master of the *will* be praised, whose design and wisdom cannot be fathomed."

Maimonides throws a new light on the concept of providence by using three prophetic terms which refer to the actions of God: ..".that I am the Lord, who exercises unfailing love, justice and righteousness in the earth" (Jeremiah 9:24), and he takes upon himself to explain how it is possible to impose commands and restrictions on man's behavior in the world, when this world is ruled by the unfailing love, justice and righteousness of God.

# XIV.

## *The Knowledge of God, the Negation of His Attributes*

Compatibilism, in a philosophical ethic which is not religious, attempts to reconcile man's free choice with the surrounding over-all determinism of natural reality, in which man himself is included. In this respect, it appears that Maimonides has the advantage, since he bases this determinism on the will of God, who establishes the laws of nature as the way of the world, and by the same will He accorded man his free choice. It is as if we were to say – following a famous Talmudic expression – that the same authority which has instituted a certain prohibition is entitled to make exceptions to this prohibition. But just where it appears to us that, in religious faith, the problem of free choice has become easier to solve, it is there that we find that it has become more difficult; and it is no accident that all the great believers have had to struggle with the problem. Atheistic determinism is concerned with nature alone, and nature – to use Maimonides' expression – "is not endowed with opinion and administration, or with thought and contemplation." Maimonides, however, bases his determinism on the will of God, who has *knowledge* – "all things are foreseen." In each of its different and even contradictory senses, the concept of free choice, when taken on the level of religious belief, would sooner or later come into conflict with the assumption of God's omniscience, *provided that the concept of God's "knowledge," in this context, is understood in human categories*, as similar to the knowledge which exists in our own mind. If I know that something is about to happen, and this

93

knowledge is true knowledge, it follows that that thing will happen; if it does not come about, then my knowledge was not true knowledge. God's knowledge is certainly true knowledge, and therefore, if the meaning of this knowledge is the same as the meaning of human knowledge and we make no distinction between our knowledge and that of God except in its extent and certainty, we are faced with an insoluble conflict. Our own knowledge is conditioned by the thing known, which precedes it of necessity in the order of time, or at least precedes it logically. I do not know except that which is, and in this respect it makes no difference whether the time of being of that which is is past, present or future. It is a mere empirical limitation on my knowledge that I do not know the future – but if I could know it, there would be no difference between my knowledge of the past and my knowledge of the future. From a logical point of view, the certainty of knowledge, in its human sense, which refers to a future event, implies the certainty that the future is already determined. If we ascribe knowledge in the same sense to God, who does not exist in time just as He does not exist in space, and whose knowledge is eternal, it follows that every voluntary decision of man, since it is already known to God, is decreed and determined from time immemorial, and we are left with no room for the possibility of choice, decision or determination by man.

Maimonides formulates this problem in its extreme as early as *The Eight Chapters*: "Does God know or does He not know that a certain individual will be good or bad? If you say 'He knows,' then it necessarily follows that man is compelled to act as God knew beforehand he would act, otherwise God's knowledge would be imperfect. If you say that God does not know in advance, then great absurdities and destructive religious theories will result."

Maimonides' decisive answer to this quandary is related to the first principle of his conception of religious faith – the negation of God's attributes. This is an issue we have mentioned time and again, but so far we have done it without a thorough examination of its philosophical significance. Maimonides' answer to this question of the conflict between God's omniscience and man's free

94

choice is that we are *not* to ascribe to God knowledge in the sense it has as a human concept. The significance of this answer for religious faith is very profound, and one should now explain it.

An important aspect of the elimination of anthropomorphism in religious faith is the negation of God's attributes; this, for Maimonides, is a precondition for the true knowledge of God and for the worship of God out of love, not out of fear – for faith for–its–own–sake rather than faith not–for–its–own–sake. This is the belief in God *qua* God, which cannot be conceived in the categories of human thought, as against the belief in God in terms of qualities and functions ascribed to Him, which are of necessity – a necessity following from the limitations of the human mind – corporeal. In our world of human consciousness, there are no qualities or functions which are not derived from the reality known to man. Thus, anyone who ascribes any such qualities to God sinks to the level of idolatry: he worships God in the image of man. The same applies even to the concept of knowledge borrowed from the human mind. It is related to a corporeal concept, whereas in fact there is nothing in common between our knowledge and the knowledge of God except the name or the term, which is used in two different senses: on the one hand, the sense known to us from our experience, and on the other, the sense which is unknown to us, which refers to the omniscience of the Creator. Our own knowledge always starts with something that is given and knowable; the knower precedes the knowledge of it. One cannot ascribe such knowledge to God, since, had He known any thing because that thing was existent, whether in the past, present or future, God would have been affected by something outside Himself. All human knowledge is derived from something which is, but God's knowledge precedes everything which exists, and everything which exists is derived from it. There is no such knowledge in the world of our consciousness and our analysis of concepts.

Maimonides attempts to remove the confrontation between man's choice and God's knowledge by negating it: this is a merely imaginary confrontation, between a concept which we define and analyze in the categories of human consciousness, and a concept about which we cannot make any statement; it is obvious, therefore, that we have no way of determining whether these two concepts can be reconciled with each other or contradict each other. Free human choice is, for Maimonides, a certain fact which he never doubts. For him, this choice is of the essence of man and is related to the idea of God's image in man. It is a postulate of faith, from which we derive the duty and the possibility of worshipping God. If it is true that many a believer has found this difficult to accept because of the concept of God's omniscience, which appears to contradict man's free choice, this is, for Maimonides, because such a believer has fallen into the logical trap of identifying God's knowledge with knowledge as a human category. Such a man raises a difficulty concerning something that is known to man from the point of view of something which is unknown and unknowable to man – the essence of God's knowledge.

This answer to the great problem, given as it appears to be in a merely negative fashion, may seem facile. But it is filled with profound significance once Maimonides attempts to clarify the meaning of the concept of "God's knowledge," which is not "knowledge" in the human sense of this term. This clarification, too, is made by negating God's attributes, based on the first principle of the belief in God's oneness. Here are Maimonides' words:

> "It is, indeed, an axiom of the science of the divine, i.e., metaphysics (and Aristotle's theory of knowledge) that God (may He be blessed!) does not know by means of knowledge" [that is, He does not know from the point of view of the given thing which He knows]... "so that He and His knowledge may be considered two different things in the sense that it is true of man; for man is distinct from knowledge" [i.e. man exists even without the knowledge he has] "and knowledge from man" [i.e. man's knowledge is not identical with man himself], "in consequence of which they are two different things. If God knew by means of knowledge, He would necessarily be a plurality." (*The Eight Chapters of Maimonides*, 8).

### The Knowledge of God, the Negation of His Attributes

A complete understanding of these words would necessitate a separate chapter on Aristotelian epistemology – the theory of knowledge of Aristotle and his followers – and the use made of it by Maimonides in his own doctrines. Within the limits we have set ourselves – to deal with Maimonides' faith, with a minimal discussion of its philosophical contents – we shall have to make do with a few hints. But let us first look at a revised version of both the question and the answer, as supplied twenty years later, in Maimonides' own language. In *Hilchot Teshuvah* 5:5, having apprised us of the great principle of man's free choice and his responsibility for all his actions, Maimonides adds, as if he is repeating what he has already said in *The Eight Chapters*: "You might ask: But the Holy one, blessed be His name, knows everything that is even before it comes into being; would he then know that this man is to be good or bad, or would he not? If he knows that this man will be good, it is impossible for this man not to be good. But if you say that it is possible for this man to be good or bad, then God has not known this properly. Understand that the answer is such that 'the measure thereof is longer than the earth, and broader than the sea,' and many great articles of faith and high mountains of religion hang by it. But you must know and understand this thing which I say, that we have already explained* that the Holy one, blessed be His name, does not know in a knowledge which is external to Himself, as do men, whose knowledge and being are two different things, but He, may His name be exalted, and His knowledge are one. Man's knowledge cannot fathom this thing, since there is no faculty in man for conceiving and revealing the truth of the Creator. This is what the prophet means when he says, 'For My thoughts are not your thoughts, neither are your ways My ways' (Isaiah 55:8). Since this is so, we have no faculty for knowing how the Holy one, blessed be His name, knows all creatures and all actions."

---

* *Yesodei ha-Torah* 2:10, which is the summary of the philosophical analysis of the conceptual triad "the knower–the known–the act of knowing": "The creator does not know and recognize these things as they exist, the way we know them, but he knows them *qua* Himself. Thus, since He knows Himself, He knows all else, because all else is dependent in its being on Him."

The philosophical analysis of this belief in divine knowledge and providence is presented extensively in *The Guide to the Perplexed*, especially 1:68 and 3:21 and 23.

We have already pointed out that this is not the place or the forum for discussing this great issue of religious philosophy, and especially so since Maimonides himself does not regard it as an end in itself. These words are directed against those who believe that it is precisely this philosophical analysis which constituted Maimonides' aim. It seems to me that philosophical analysis was, in the hands of Maimonides, only an instrument for purifying the belief in God from the dross of human imagery, which smells of idolatry. A recognition of "the Lord is One" makes it incumbent upon us to remove from Him any attributes which originate of necessity in our own concepts – concepts derived from our cognizance of natural reality, our own reality. If we understand such attributes in their human sense, we make the creator similar to His creation – or, in the expression of our Talmudic Sages, we "assimilate the form to its former." If, as we do, we find the language of religious discourse – both in the Bible and the literature of the Sages and the language of our prayers – abounding in attributes of God, we should understand these as a consequence of the limited language of human beings, in which the Torah speaks. They are justified when used as auxiliary means for religious thought, to prevent man from speaking evil of his God. But the truth of the matter is that one cannot separate God from His attributes, the way we can separate man, who is the substrate of these attributes, from his own attributes. Knowledge is included among these attributes. Therefore – to use Maimonides' own expression – "just as we cannot comprehend the truth of His essence, but at the same time we know that His being is more perfect than all being... thus, although we do not know the truth of His knowledge, since it is identical with His essence, we do know... that neither a multiplicity of insights nor the acquisition of new insights pertains to Him." This is unlike man's knowledge, whose contents are renewed and segmented, the more man observes what exists and learns from it.

Belief in God in the sense of His Godhead, with regard to his being God, and not with regard to functions ascribed to Him – which is true naive faith, not the faith of those who pretend to be naive – is in no way dependent on a certain understanding of God, just as it is in no way dependent on a certain understanding of His providence. Both constitute theological and philosophical problems for the believer, but they are not the content of his belief. The pinnacle of faith is reached by Maimonides in his comments on the Book of Job, to which we have already referred in one of the earlier chapters. In the sequel to his words concerning *providence*, which we have quoted there, he connects it with *knowledge*. This is what he says of both of them: "This lesson is the principal object of the whole book of Job; it lays down the principle of faith and recommends us to derive a proof from nature, that we should not fall into the error of imagining His knowledge to be similar to ours, or His intention, providence, and rule similar to ours. When we know this, we shall find everything which may befall us easy to bear; mishap will create no doubts in our hearts concerning God, whether He knows our affairs or not, whether He provides for us or abandons us. On the contrary, our fate will *increase our love of God.*" (*Guide* 3:23).

This "love of God" is faith itself. The faith that is in the heart of the true believer – such as Abraham on Mount Moriah and Job after he came to know God – is not an answer he gives himself to questions concerning God's ways with this world or man's destiny, which are all questions relevant only to man's care for his own welfare. Faith is man's willingness to worship God in the world as it is.

Maimonides makes Job the mouthpiece for his own faith:

Job gives up his view [concerning Divine providence] which was most mistaken and recognizes that he had been mistaken therein ... He said all that he did say so long as he had no true knowledge and knew God only because of his acceptance of authority, just as the multitude of the believers know him. But when he knew God with a certain knowledge, he admitted that true happiness, which is the knowledge of

99

God, is guaranteed to all who know him and that a human being cannot be troubled in it by any or all the misfortunes in question. While he had only known through the traditional stories and by the way of reflection, Job had imagined that the things thought to be happiness, such as health, wealth, and children, are the ultimate goal. For this reason he fell into such perplexity and said such things as he did ... It is because of his final discourse indicative of correct apprehension that it is said of him: "For you have not spoken of Me, the being that is right, as my servant Job has." (*Guide* 3:23).

# XV.

## *The Commandments of the Torah*

In the world of the faith of Maimonides, the great question of providence, divine knowledge and human choice is solved because the believer does not ask himself how God knows him, but how he knows God – "And in accordance with a man's knowledge of God will be his love of God" – these are the final words of *Sefer ha-Mada* in *Mishneh Torah*. In *The Guide for the Perplexed*, the formulation is "Knowledge of God is the comprehension of God" – that is, it is not the knowledge God has of man, but the comprehension attained by man of God.

What follows on this comprehension of God by man? Here, too, Maimonides brings about something like a Copernican revolution in faith by reducing it to its true essence. Comprehension of God is the undertaking man imposes on himself – an undertaking to worship God. The true believer knows that the acceptance of this undertaking, which originates within himself, is the gift with which he has been endowed by God. God has endowed him with the faculty of worshipping Him. Here we have reached one of the largest issues of the faith of Maimonides – the interpretation of the practical commandments. It is most likely that this issue, in the whole of Maimonides' thought, is of the greatest importance to the believer of today, who is no longer living within the world of Aristotelian philosophical thought. This issue is related to religious existence even today. We have already emphasized time and again, as against some other interpretations, that Maimonides is the man of the *halachah*, the Jew of the *halachah*, of the great complex of practical commandments which is the religious program for every-day life.

What is the significance of the practical commandments against the background of that faith whose fundaments we have endcavored to explain in all the previous chapters? Maimonides defines and explains it in the clearest manner by means of the great distinction between the two levels of divine worship – the level of worship "for–its–own–sake" and the level of worship "not–for–its–own–sake," the final level and the instrumental level (*Commentary on the Mishnah, Sanhedrin*, Ch. *Helek*). The worship of God by fulfilling the practical commandments is the final aim, since the man who recognizes God has nothing to which he can attach a significance of value except the worship of God.

But before man can reach the rank signified and symbolized by Abraham's standing before God on Mount Moriah, he has to pass through a long and tortuous course of education, of overcoming the impulsive and the imaginative forces within him. One of the most interesting issues in Maimonides' anthropology is the identification he makes between the impulsive elements and the imaginative elements in man's consciousness. A man must, first of all, overcome the imaginative powers and the impulsive powers within himself, in order to direct his consciousness toward a cognition of God in the realm of objective reality in which he has been placed, and which is an inseparable part of his personality. Maimonides does not follow in the way of those thinkers who separate man's spiritual or physical world from his life as flesh and blood. These two are inseparable. Man is one, and his biological, social and intellectual functions are all derived from the various "powers" or "potencies" of his *one* soul. Therefore, man cannot strive toward his final aim, which is the realization of his intellectual faculty for the purpose of recognizing God, unless he realizes his other faculties in accordance with this purpose. It is true that the activity of these faculties can do nothing more than satisfy man's needs as a biological creature and arrange his affairs as a social animal; yet this satisfaction and this arrangement are necessary conditions for the direction of his intellectual faculty toward the attainment of that which is beyond these needs and affairs – knowledge of God, and man's standing before God.

The road leading man to his perfection is the Torah and its commandments. The Torah has two aims: the "welfare of the body" and the "welfare of the soul" – the former being instrumental, the latter final (*Guide* 3:27–28). The "emendation of the body" does not consist of hygiene and medicine (which are, in any case, an existential necessity), but in morality and the life of the state (ethics and politics) – the proper channelling of man's impulsive and imaginative powers and the regulation of the interactions between people.

The "emendation of the body" is the subjection of all other faculties of man's soul to his intellectual faculties – but this is not in itself the purpose of man. Here we discover clearly the chasm which separates the scale of values of religious belief from that of non-religious humanism. What Maimonides calls the "emendation of the body" – man's morality and the perfection of human society – is, for the humanist, the purpose which man ought to attain, and if he has attained it, he has reached his perfection. For Maimonides, this has only an instrumental significance, not the significance of value. We cannot ascribe a significance of value to human existence, which is not true being. God alone is true being, and therefore no value can be attached to man's attainments in this world except to the recognition of God and the attachment to Him. This is not to say that Maimonides despises the "emendation of the body," but merely that he regards it as a means, and not as an end in itself. The end is the "emendation of the soul." This is the name given by Maimonides to the attainment of the intellectual faculty in man when it has reached the recognition of the truth – which is the recognition of God.

Of this final aim, Maimonides has made a penetrating observation which has created much consternation, and even acrimony and opposition, among people who regard themselves with all sincerity as believers, but find it difficult to comprehend Maimonides' faith. These are his words: "Man's final perfection does not consist of actions or moral behavior, but in opinions alone." The "opinions" spoken of here are nothing but the recognition of God, since any other opinion, even if it is correct in itself, is an opinion concerning something which is not true being. The purpose is knowledge of God, and the meaning of the statement that it "does not consist of actions or moral behavior," is not that the man who has attained this end has freed himself of actions and morality (as maintained by some modern systems of thought: that the perfect man is beyond good and evil and everything is permissible to him). What Maimonides means is that the actions and qualities which are necessary for the perfection of man are not perfection itself. He distinguishes between "that which is prior in importance" and "that which is prior in nature and in the order of time." The perfection of the body is prior in nature and time; man has first to perfect himself from the moral point of view and to perfect the society within which he lives, and which, of necessity, affects him. Only then will it be possible for him to have leisure and devote his faculties to the "emendation of the soul." But from the point of view of its importance, the emendation of the soul is prior to the emendation of the body.

What is the way in which man performs these emendations? The emendations of the body consist of the practical commandments, all of which are interpreted by Maimonides, in the first stage of his detailed discussion of the reasons for the commandments (*Guide* 3:29–49), as educational means – whether for the removal of obstacles in man's way toward perfection (chief of which is the *eradication of idolatry*), or for his moral or social emendation. In a discussion of the practical commandments *on this level*, he says: "and all these things are in order to subdue man's impulses and to emend his characteristics; and most of the laws of the Torah are nothing but "counsels from afar by the One who is great in counsel," for the sake of emending man's characteristics and rectifying all his actions" (*Mishneh Torah, Hilchot Temurah* 4:3). The emendation of the body is a religious duty, although it is worship of God not–for–its–own–sake; for it goes without saying that social perfection is for the sake of man – but even moral perfection is no more than man's improvement for the sake of man.

The atheist humanist Kant, who regards man himself as the supreme value, sees the purpose in man's improvement for his own sake. Maimonides does not regard this as the purpose, but merely as a necessary means. Only once he has perfected his body can man turn himself to the emendation of his soul; and, if he invests in this emendation the whole of his voluntary and intellectual powers, he may attain to the true belief in God, which is knowledge of God. From the vantage point of this knowledge of God, the commandments of God are then conceived in an entirely different manner.

What does a man conclude from his knowledge of God? He can reach only one conclusion: that he must worship God – that is, attach himself to God, since He is truth and He is being. What, then, is the worship of God? The fulfillment of God's commandments. Here we have an amazing dialectic. In the first place, the commandments have been presented as a means for making it possible for man to reach his purpose. This means is necessary since Maimonides, in his profound realism, in his vision of man as an integral whole, not as a combination of a spiritual complex and a bodily complex, recognizes that "a man will not comprehend the truth and will not perform good acts when he is ill or hungry or fleeing his enemies." The emendation of the body is necessary, and the commandments of the Torah direct man toward this emendation. When a man has achieved this emendation of his body, he can turn to the emendation of his soul, and from now on it is entirely up to him – to his intellectual and voluntary powers – whether he is to reach his final end, which is knowledge of God, indicated by the Torah. Once he has reached that point, man recognizes that God must be worshipped – that is, one has to fulfill for the sake of God those very commandments which he has previously fulfilled for his own sake. Having provided us with the systematic interpretation, in all its great and small details, of every single one of the 613 commandments in the Torah, which are interpreted by Maimonides with regard to their importance for the moral education of man and for the regulation of inter-personal relations, Maimonides moves to another level in his conception of the significance of the commandments, and asserts: "We must bear in mind that all such religious acts... and the performance of... precepts, serve exclusively as the means of causing us to occupy and fill our mind with the precepts of God."

This sentence seems to be paradoxical. From its first words it appears that the practical commandments are a means to a certain intellectual purpose – but the very purpose to which this means leads us is revealed to be nothing but the idea of the performance of these commandments. Maimonides continues: "... to occupy and fill our minds with the precepts of God, *and free us from worldly business*." But worldly business is, after all, the emendation of the body! Worldly business is necessary, but it is not the final aim. Here Maimonides reaches the pinnacle of pure faith: "... *for we are thus, as it were, occupied with God, and not with any other thing*." (*Guide* 3:51).

The fulfillment of the commandments does not have, as its final aim, human perfection, although the perfection of man is necessary in order to make it possible for man to worship God. Nor is its aim the perfection of society, although the perfection of human society is necessary in order to make it possible for man to worship God. The final aim of fulfilling the commandments is that man should occupy himself with God. In his rationalization of the commandments, in interpreting them by educational, moral or social reasons, Maimonides was aiming merely at that level of faith on which man can only reach the worship of God not–for–its–own–sake. If the level of man's faith is such that he must ask questions like: Why was such or such commandment given? Why do I perform it? we explain to him that this commandment was given for the perfection of morals, of society or the like. But when a man has reached a cognition of the truth, he understands that "occupying oneself with God" – that is, performing the commandments, not because they have reasons in relation to man, but because they are the commands of God – this in itself is the final aim.

We are now in a position to understand why Maimonides, to whom "perfection" is embodied in intellectual attainment, is attached to the practical commandments by the profoundest *spiritual* attachment. This attachment finds its expression in remarks which he makes in the course of his discussion of *halachic*, legal and technical matters. Let us take a few examples: "It is proper for a man to contemplate the laws of the sacred Torah and reach as perfect an understanding of them as is in his power; and if he has found one of them, for which he can detect no cause or reason, he should not make light of it or think of it as he thinks of other, profane, matters ... For one should not kick against commandments legislated for us by the Holy One, blessed be His name, even if one does not know their reason, and one should not ascribe to God things which are not thus, and not think his thoughts concerning them as he thinks of matters profane..." (*Mishneh Torah, Meilah* 8:8); "A man should pay attention to the *mezuzah* since it is incumbent on everyone always, and whenever he goes in or out of his house he will meet with the uniqueness of the name of the Holy One and remind himself of His love, and awaken from his sleep and his errors in matters temporal, and he will know that there is nothing which stands for ever and ever except the knowledge of the Rock of the world, and he will immediately revert to his right mind and walk in the ways of righteousness. Our early Sages have said: 'Anyone who has *tefillin* on his head and arm and *tzitzit* on his garment and a *mezuzah* on his doorpost – he can be certain not to sin'" (Bab. *Menahot* 43b). Maimonides interprets this Talmudic saying: "For he has many reminders, and these are the angels who save him from sinning, as it is written (Psalms 34:7), 'The angel of the Lord encamps round about them that fear him, and delivers them'" (*ibid.*, *Mezuzah* 6:10).

With the recognition that Maimonides' discussion of faith and of the worship of God is a discussion on two levels – that of Torah for–its–own–sake and that of Torah not–for–its–own–sake – the artificial distinction between "Maimonides the philosopher" and "Maimonides the man of the *halachah*" has been cancelled.

# XVI.

## *The Torah – a Torah for Every Man*

Maimonides emphasizes time and again that true faith was the cognition attained by Moses, and this is why the Bible ascribes to him a knowledge of God "face to face." The realization of such faith in life was the standing of Abraham on Mount Moriah, and this is why he was told: "...now I know that you fear God" (Gen. 22:12).

Some people describe Maimonides' faith as elitist – a faith directed toward the few elect and toward them alone. Maimonides would not deny that. He makes a sharp distinction between "man" and "the perfect man," and his faith is the faith of the perfect man. But Maimonides is no elitist in the sense of distinguishing between men who were destined by their very nature to be perfect and others who have been denied this faculty. On the contrary, he makes the courageous assertion: "*Each man* is worthy of being as righteous as our Teacher Moses" (*Hilchot Teshuvah* 5:2). But he is also aware that not every man is capable of that psychical heroism required for realizing the potential inherent in him and bringing his abilities into realization. Maimonides knows that the Torah takes account of the weakness of man and that it *allows* men "to worship God in the hope of reward and to abstain from transgression for fear of punishment." That is to say that the worship of God not–for–its–own–sake is not disallowed. Even a man who occupies himself with Torah not–for–its–own–sake is worshipping God; he is a man, and he is a Jew. Maimonides accepts the view of those Talmudic Sages who maintained that occupying oneself with Torah not–for–its–own–sake is likely, through its educational effect, to lead a man to Torah for–its–own–sake – as against the view of other Sages who were stricter, and called Torah for–its–own–sake an elixir of life for man, and Torah not–for–its–own–sake a death potion. The final aim is to walk in the ways of Abraham our Father; but Maimonides does not require of every single man to walk that way. He says: "Toward that way a man should *awaken himself*" (Introduction to commentary on *Helek*) – a man should *endeavor* to walk that way. If he endeavors to do so, the Torah recognizes him as a man who has worshipped God, even if he has not reached that final aim, which only those "that excel in strength, that do his commandments" can attain. This accords with the words of our Sages at the end of *Avot* (5:26): "According to the labor is the reward." Worthiness is measured, not by attainment, but by the effort which a man makes in order to reach the attainment; or – as Maimonides has it: "according to the worth of your labor in the Torah will be your reward."

If the worship of God *for–its–own–sake* – which on the face of it is an extremely arduous demand imposed on man's consciousness – is recognized as the purpose of religion whether the individual believer is capable of attaining to it, or his faith remains only an effort to attain it, the way is open to *every* man, in *every* historical period, and through *every* change and mutation in civilization and culture. Such an understanding of religious faith liberates us from any dependence on the information available to man concerning his natural and historical reality and from our dependence on any complex of values, beliefs and opinions current among the public in any generation, even if the believer himself is part of that public. The worship of God not–for–its–own–sake, however – although it appears to be easier with regard to man's consciousness – is of necessity dependent on such information and on such values. If religion is "for the sake of man" – in any of the senses of this formula: whether for the material or spiritual utility and well-being of man; for satisfying his psychological need or his demand to understand the world, nature and history; or for the perfection of man and society, for "the redemption of man" (or "the redemption of Israel") – faith is turned into "a love which depends on some external cause," and it is destined to be like any other such love. As soon as the conception of the needs and values of man has changed, or as soon as man has acquired new and different information concerning the world, nature or history, such a faith is likely to be undermined. But the belief in God *qua* God, and not as to the contribution made by religion to man's needs and interests, is "love which does not depend on an external cause." Such a belief is embodied in the Torah and the *mitzvot*, and no new reality or cognition of reality would be able to undermine it, since these are irrelevant to it. The difference between these two religious approaches can be formulated thus: a faith which consists of the information in the hands of man – or the information he thinks he possesses – concerning his God and His relation to the world, as against a faith which consists of a man's knowledge of himself with regard to his duty toward his God. Here we have reached an understanding of what appears to be a paradox in the faith of Maimonides.

The religious thought of Maimonides appears to be embedded and enshrined in a particular world view – the cosmology and physics of ancient and medieval "science" – and in certain categories of thought – the ontology, logic and epistemology of Aristotle and his followers. For this reason, his thought is held to be a "religious philosophy." This world view and these methods of thinking have not stood the test of time, and today they are not part of our spiritual world. But out of Maimonides' spiritual world one can distill what we have called "the faith of Maimonides," and this faith is revealed to us – albeit without Maimonides' own intention – with a vigor and forcefulness which are in no way dependent on the philosophical apparatus by means of which it was originally expressed. What is more, it is far more vigorous than any other system of belief in what is held to be "naive" Judaism, whose believers could not reach a cognition of God except inasmuch as He is the one who administers the world – that is, the believing man himself; that is – a belief in God from the point of view of man. Such were most of the systems of belief in Judaism.* As against them, for Maimonides "The Lord is God." It is in this sense that I put forward, at the very beginning of this volume, the claim that Maimonides' image should be seen, not only as the image of the greatest of *halachic* authorities in Israel, or that of the greatest of the philosophers of the religion of Israel, but chiefly as that of the greatest of all believers after the Patriarchs and the Prophets. "From Moses to Moses there was none like Moses."

---

* One can see this in the Kabbalah and in its ramifications in the Hassidic movement, for whom God "invests himself" in the world – hence the *Sefirot*, the *Partzufim*, and the like.